To Grace -

Thank you for your
interest in my research!

Laurel :)

8/21

The Partisan Gap

Why Democratic Women Get Elected
But Republican Women Don't

Laurel Elder

NEW YORK UNIVERSITY PRESS

New York

NEW YORK UNIVERSITY PRESS
New York
www.nyupress.org

References to Internet websites (URLs) were accurate at the time of writing. Neither the author nor New York University Press is responsible for URLs that may have expired or changed since the manuscript was prepared.

Library of Congress Cataloging-in-Publication Data
Names: Elder, Laurel, author.
Title: The partisan gap : why Democratic women get elected but Republican women don't / Laurel Elder.
Other titles: Why Democratic women get elected but Republican women do not
Description: New York : NEW YORK UNIVERSITY PRESS, [2021] | Includes bibliographical references and index.
Identifiers: LCCN 2020048480 | ISBN 9781479804818 (Hardback : acid-free paper) | ISBN 9781479804825 (Paperback : acid-free paper) | ISBN 9781479804849 (eBook) | ISBN 9781479804870 (eBook Other)
Subjects: LCSH: Political parties—United States—Platforms. | Democratic Party (U.S.)—History. | Liberalism—United States—History. | Republican Party (U.S. : 1854–)—History. | Conservatism—United States—History. | Political culture—United States—History. | Legislators—Recruiting—United States. | Minorities—Political activity—United States—History. | Women—Political activity—United States—History. | Women legislators—United States—History. | Women political candidates—United States.
Classification: LCC JK2255 .E66 2021b | DDC 324.273—dc23
LC record available at https://lccn.loc.gov/2020048480

New York University Press books are printed on acid-free paper, and their binding materials are chosen for strength and durability. We strive to use environmentally responsible suppliers and materials to the greatest extent possible in publishing our books.

Manufactured in the United States of America

10 9 8 7 6 5 4 3 2 1

Also available as an ebook

CONTENTS

PREFACE

The analyses for this book were completed in summer 2020, as anticipation was building for the 2020 elections. While no woman ran as either party's presidential nominee, Kamala Harris was elected in November 2020 as the first woman vice president of the United States. The 2020 elections also saw a record number of women run and win legislative office, shattering the records set in 2018.

Yet, the story of women's representation in elective office is a tale of two parties. For the past several decades, Democratic women have made steady, impressive gains in state legislatures and Congress, and they are on a clear path toward equal representation among their party's elected officials. Progress for Republican women, however, has stalled and in many cases reversed, leaving the Republican party-in-government more male-dominated today than three decades ago. As a result of these contrasting partisan dynamics, as of 2020, there are five times as many Democratic women in Congress as Republican women.

This book argues that the causes of the dramatic partisan gap among women in elective office are not short-term or idiosyncratic but grounded in structural forces that have reshaped the American party system over the last half century. The racial, ideological, and regional realignments of the Democratic and Republican parties—transformations that have received widespread discussion in scholarly literature as well as the popular press—have also had a tremendous impact on women's representation, which has received far less attention. These structural changes to the American political landscape have resulted in favorable opportunities for the advancement of a diverse group of Democratic women and a more challenging and unwelcoming environment for Republican women office seekers.

The argument advanced in this book suggests that the gains made by women in elective office in future election cycles will primarily be driven by Democratic women and will result in the continuation of the already dramatic partisan gap among women in state legislatures and Congress. The partisan gap among women officials is driven by the broad structural forces shaping contemporary American politics. As a result, the strikingly different levels of representation of Republican and Democratic women in elective office is unlikely to meaningfully abate until there is a new party realignment that reshapes the party coalitions and electoral environment in the United States.

Introduction

The Partisan Dynamics of Women's Representation

There are many compelling reasons to be concerned about women's underrepresentation in elective political office. Women compose slightly more than 50 percent of the population in the United States but remain dramatically underrepresented in all types of elective political office, from state legislatures, to Congress, to governorships. The United States has yet to elect a woman as president. Many believe American democracy would be healthier and stronger if its elected officials were a more accurate reflection of the public.

Having women descriptively represented in political office allows women and girls to see people like themselves in positions of power and lends legitimacy to the political system.[1] Women carry out their work as elected officials differently than men. They bring a distinctive set of priorities and operate differently than their male colleagues driven by their distinctive experiences as women, and thus the underrepresentation of women holds significant consequences for substantive representation.[2] Women's representation in state- and national-level political institutions is particularly important as legislatures are passing, or attempting to pass, laws concerning health care, reproductive rights, sexual assault, pay equity, and the minimum wage, issues that disproportionately and differentially affect women. Moreover, having more women in elective office may help our political institutions function more effectively and better address our nation's problems.[3]

For those who value women's representation and believe that our democracy would be stronger if women were represented proportionally, the past several decades have been frustrating. Women's representation in political office has increased only at a very slow rate. In fact, in some years, the number of women in the US House of Representatives and in state legislatures actually went down, challenging the assumption that progress toward equal representation by gender might be slow but would inevitably happen.

The 2018 elections marked a departure from this glacial progress as women smashed existing records for political office holding. The 116th Congress (2019–2021) has within it a record-breaking 26 women in the Senate and 101 women in the House of Representatives.[4] Women also made history in state legislatures, making a net gain of 256 seats. Women now form 29 percent of state legislators nationally. As of 2020, there are also nine women governors (18 percent of all governors), which ties an earlier record for the most women governors serving simultaneously.[5]

Behind the good news about women's increased representation in elected office is another story, one about the political parties and the different experiences women are having within them as office seekers and members of the party-in-government. While women's representation in elective office is at an all-time high, the size of the partisan gap between the representation of Democratic women and Republican women is also record-breaking. Today, an overwhelming majority of women in elective office are

Democrats, while Republicans form a small and, in many cases, shrinking portion of women in elective office.

An overwhelming 83 percent of the women in the 116th Congress are Democrats, while just 17 percent are Republicans. Put another way, there are more than four times as many Democratic women in Congress than Republican women. A large partisan gap also characterizes women's representation in state legislatures. Democratic women compose 68 percent of women state legislators, while Republican women form less than one-third.[6] While women in society overall are somewhat more likely to affiliate as Democrats than Republicans, the partisan gap among women elected officials far exceeds the partisan gap among women in the electorate. The magnitude of the partisan gap among women in Congress and state legislatures is all the more dramatic considering it is a relatively new feature of American politics. Until the 1990s, women in elected office were equally likely to be Republicans and Democrats.

The dramatic partisan gap among women in political office today is the product of two contrasting dynamics characterizing the trajectory of women elected officials within the two parties—steady progress for Democratic women contrasted against stalled and in some cases reversed progress for Republican women.

Democratic Women on Steady Upward Trajectory

For decades, Democratic women have made steady gains in state legislatures, the US House of Representatives, and the US Senate. As a result, women form 38 percent of Democrats in the House and 36 percent of Democrats in the Senate in the 116th Congress. While women have not attained parity with men among Democratic elected officials, they are on a clear trajectory to do so.

Democratic women now hold key leadership positions within Congress, most notably the position of Speaker of the House, held by Representative Nancy Pelosi, as well as eleven other leadership roles in the House and five leadership roles in the Senate, including the position of assistant majority leader held by Senator Patty Murray.[7] A number of Democratic women officeholders have taken on highly prominent roles in the national media due to their 2020 presidential election bids, including Senator Kamala Harris, Senator Elizabeth Warren, Senator Amy Klobuchar, Senator Kirsten Gillibrand, and Representative Tulsi Gabbard.

Democratic women in Congress have increased in terms of their numbers and their national visibility, and they have also become a markedly more diverse group in terms of race and ethnicity. The 2018 midterms saw a number of historic firsts, including the election of Ilhan Omar and Rashida Tlaib, the first two Muslim American women elected to Congress (Omar is also the first Somali American and refugee from the continent of Africa to serve in Congress, and Tlaib is the first Palestinian American to serve);[8] Sharice Davids and Deb Haaland, the first Native American women elected to Congress; Jahana Hayes, the first Black woman to represent Connecticut in Congress; Ayanna Pressley, the first Black woman to represent Massachusetts in Congress; Veronica Escobar and Sylvia Garcia, the first Latinx women to represent Texas in Congress; and Alexandria Ocasio-Cortez (AOC), a Latina who also holds the distinction of being the youngest woman ever elected to Congress.[9] Four of these newly elected members of Congress—Ilhan Omar, Rashida Tlaib, Ayanna

Pressley, and Alexandria Ocasio-Cortez—a group collectively known as "the squad," have received very high levels of national attention for their progressive politics and clashes with President Trump over his policies and nativist rhetoric. What is notable about all of these path-breaking women is that they are all Democrats. Women of color now compose 43 percent of the Democratic women in Congress. In summary, this diverse group of Democratic women, through their strong numbers, their leadership positions, and their high levels of visibility, are well-positioned to influence strategy, policy, and deliberation among Democrats in Congress.

The steady progress of Democratic women can also be seen in state legislatures across the country. Election after election, women increased their representation among Democratic state legislators (see figure 2.1). Heading into the 2020 elections, women formed 42 percent of Democratic state legislators nationally. In ten states women actually form *a majority of Democratic state legislators* (see table 2.1). In other words, women in the Democratic party-in-government have exceeded all notions of critical mass to actually form the majority voice in their party's caucus in one-fifth of state legislatures. The Democratic women in state legislatures are also highly diverse, with women of color forming 36 percent of the group.[10] As of 2020, Democratic women also hold fifty-five leadership positions in state senates and state houses across the nation.[11]

Stalled and Reversed Progress for Republican Women

A strikingly different dynamic characterizes the elective office-holding trends of Republican women. Women's representation among Republican state legislators reached its high point in the early 1990s and then started going down (see figure 2.1). In a surprise to those who assumed women's representation in elective office would inevitably increase with time, women actually form a smaller share of Republican state legislators today than they did in the early 1990s. In contrast to their Democratic counterparts, Republican women state legislators are not diverse in terms of race and ethnicity. Slightly more than 97 percent of Republican women state legislators are white.[12] While there are fifty-five Democratic women holding leadership positions in state legislatures, there are only twenty Republican women in such positions.[13]

Republican women have also struggled to maintain, let alone increase, their representation in Congress. In 2005, there were twenty-nine Republican women in Congress, yet as of January 2019 that number had dwindled to twenty-one (see figure 3.1). The struggle of Republican women is illustrated vividly in the 2018 election outcomes, which resulted in the number of Republican women in the US House of Representatives dropping from twenty-three to a mere thirteen. Women compose only 8 percent of Republicans in Congress, less than they did two decades ago (see figure 3.2). In direct contrast to their Democratic counterparts, Republican women in Congress have not become a more diverse group. In the 116th Congress, all Republican women in the Senate are white, and all the Republican women in the House are white except one, Representative Jaime Herrera Beutler from Washington, who is Latinx. There is only one Republican woman in a leadership position in the 116th House and only one Republican woman in a leadership position in the Senate.[14] Thus, Republican women form a very white, very small, and shrinking voice within the Republican party-in-government.

The emergence of the partisan gap among women in elected office and the stalled progress of Republican women are surprising for a number of reasons. While there are more women who identify as Democrats than Republicans, there are millions and millions of Republican women who could, in theory, run for political office. According to exit polls, 42 percent of women voted for Republican Donald Trump in the 2016 presidential election, and 40 percent of women voted for Republican candidates in the 2018 congressional election, illustrating that although they are outnumbered by Democratic women, there exists a huge pool of potential Republican women candidates. In many states, particularly in the South, there are more women who identify as Republican and vote for Republican candidates than there are women who identify as Democrats. It is also important to note that women's partisanship over the late twentieth century moved in the opposite direction of the partisan gap among women in elective office, with women becoming less Democratic.[15]

Another reason the partisan gap among women elected officials is surprising is that it has emerged across the same period that women have made tremendous progress in educational and professional attainment.[16] Since the early 1990s, women have graduated from college at higher rates than men. Women are attending law school and entering legal careers, which are common launching pads for political careers, at similar rates as men.[17] In other words, women have been steadily increasing their presence among what scholars have labeled the eligibility pool of candidates—individuals who possess the informal requirements of political officeholders, including high levels of education, law degrees, and experience in professions, most notably lawyers, that often act as launching pads for political careers.[18] Many predicted that as women's presence within the candidate eligibility pool increased, women's presence among those in elective office would also increase. This has happened, as the following chapters of the book illustrate, but only for Democratic women. Surprisingly, the growing pool of highly educated women, with a range of relevant professional experiences, has not turned into increasing representation for Republican women in elective office. In fact, over the same time that women have made significant gains professionally and in terms of education, the number of Republican women in elected office has stalled and in many cases gone down.

The dwindling number of Republican women in elected office at the state and national levels is also surprising given the robust, policy-oriented, grassroots activism and leadership among conservative women over the last several decades. While women have been active within the Republican Party and conservative causes across the twentieth century, political scientist Ronnee Schreiber documents how conservative women's organizations became particularly active in the 1980s, advocating for a range of policies that they viewed as helping women and families.[19] With the emergence and prominence of the Tea Party movement in the twenty-first century, conservative women became what scholar Melissa Deckman refers to as a "visible force with which to be reckoned."[20] Yet, this grassroots activism by traditionally conservative as well as Tea Party women has not resulted in significant inroads into state- or national-level elective office by Republican women. On the contrary, the Republican party-in-government is more male-dominated today than in prior decades.

Finally, the lack of progress for Republican women in political office is surprising because it has occurred across a period in which the Republican Party has flourished at the national and state levels. Although 2018 was not a good year for Republican office seekers, in the three decades prior, Republicans made historic gains. Republicans emerged from the 2016 elections in control of sixty-seven state legislative chambers, the most the party has held throughout its history, as well as more than 4,160 state legislative seats, the most the Republican Party has held since 1920. Republicans also emerged from the 2016 elections with thirty-three governorships, more than at any time since 1922.[21] On the national level, Republicans emerged from the 2014 elections with their largest majority in Congress since the late 1920s.[22] Yet, as Republicans amassed power, seized openings, and turned legislative seats from blue to red, women in the party were not able to use these strategic opportunities to increase their presence among Republican elected officials. Republican wave elections, such as in 2010 and 2014, had no meaningful effect on women's level of representation among Republican legislators at the state or national level. Republican women came away from these red tidal wave elections just as marginalized among their Republican colleagues as they had been previously.

Understanding the Partisan Gap among Women in Elective Office

Why has such a dramatic partisan gap emerged among women in political office over the past three decades?

What factors and processes have propelled the steady progress of Democratic women in elected office? And why are Republican women struggling to increase their numbers, and even withering in terms of their levels of representation? This book seeks to explain the different dynamics of women's representation in elected political office across the two major political parties. The following chapters explore the role of several interconnected developments in American electoral politics—the ideological polarization of the parties; the evolving regional bases of the parties; the intersection of race, ethnicity, and gender; and the parties' contrasting approaches to recruitment—in contributing to the markedly different partisan dynamics shaping women's representation.

Understanding the reasons behind the partisan gap is crucial to understanding why women remain underrepresented in positions of political power in the United States, and what can be done to increase women's representation. Researchers have explored a number of reasons for why women remain underrepresented in elective office, including gender differences in political ambition;[23] the challenges of fundraising;[24] the power of incumbency in reproducing white male power;[25] and bias against women candidates by party officials, campaign donors, and voters.[26] The reality, though, is that we cannot fully understand women's continued underrepresentation, or progress, in elective office in the United States without centering our analyses on the two political parties that dominate politics and structure every facet of American elections, from candidate emergence to voting behavior. As the statistics reviewed show, the dynamics of women's political office holding varies dramatically across the two parties. There is something very different happening when it comes to women candidates and women elected officials in the Democratic Party compared with their Republican counterparts. Only by carefully examining the factors helping and hindering women's representation within each party, separately and comparatively, as this book does, can we develop a full and accurate understanding of women in elective office today.

The ideological polarization of the parties, the regional changes in the geographic bases of the parties, and the political incorporation of Americans of color combined with the realignment of the parties over issues of race and civil rights have dramatically restructured American politics in ways that have been explored extensively by scholars. These structural and in many cases seismic changes to American electoral politics and party coalitions have also had another profound impact that has received less attention, and that impact has been on the representation of women, and more specifically on the emergence and growth of the partisan gap among women in political office. The central argument of this book is that as the parties have realigned regionally, ideologically, and in terms of race, they have created the conditions for Democratic women to make steady progress, while making the path for Republican women office seekers much harder.

Put another way, the partisan gap among women in elective office is not a short-term phenomenon but rather the product of long-term changes in the electoral and party system. One implication of this argument is that shorter-term factors, such as the election of Republican Donald Trump as president in 2016 and the emergence of the #MeToo movement, both of which have brought sustained attention to issues of sexual harassment, assault, and gender differentials in power, are not central causes of the partisan gap among women in office. There is evidence that Trump's election contributed to the record number of Democratic women who ran for office in 2018;[27] thus, in that way his presidency has accelerated the growth of the partisan gap. Moreover, the embrace of white identity and white nationalism by President Trump may be widening the partisan gap among women in elected office by further realigning the parties over racial and ethnic lines.[28] Yet President Trump's election alone did not cause the partisan gap among women in office, and it stands to follow that Donald Trump's exit from the presidency will not close the partisan gap or reverse the downward trajectory of Republican women in elective office. The long-term, structural forces driving the partisan gap will remain at work beyond Trump's presidency as well as through the peaks and valleys in mobilization related to the #MeToo movement.

The goal of this book, which is to better understand the structural causes of the partisan gap, is vitally important for a number of reasons. The growing partisan gap holds consequences for the future of women's representation, for policy debates and outcomes, and for the parties' future recruitment efforts and ultimately for their viability as major parties in the twenty-first century. There is no path for women to achieve proportional representation and hence gender equality in elective office without women's representation increasing in both the Democratic Party and the Republican Party. Moreover, conservative and Republican women have policy priorities and perspectives on issues that are distinctive from those of conservative and Republican men. Without women gaining meaningful representation among Republicans in elective office, their distinctive views are not able to shape Republican Party priorities and policy outcomes. Having more Republican women in elective office would likely lead the Republican Party to approach both politics and policy differently. The partisan gap among women in elective office is also of vital importance to the political parties themselves. In interviews with me as well as with national press outlets, a number of Republican Party elites have described recruiting and electing more women as, quite simply, a matter of party survival.[29]

Overview of the Book

The remainder of this chapter provides an overview of the book, describing how it proceeds from theoretical frameworks to exploring empirical evidence about women's office holding at the state and national levels, to exploring the broader implications of the partisan gap.

Chapter 1 outlines the four theoretical frameworks used to assess the emergence and causes of the partisan gaps among women in elective office in the United States: evolving party ideologies; the regional realignment of the parties; the intersection of race, ethnicity, gender, and partisanship; and finally the impact of the parties' distinct cultures on the recruitment of women office seekers. The book then draws on these four theoretical frameworks, and the specific hypotheses they generate, to assess the causes of the partisan gap among women officeholders in state legislatures (chapter 2) and the US Congress (chapters 3 and 4).

The first theoretical framework relates to the evolving ideologies of the two major parties. It is grounded in the argument that over the past several decades the parties have changed ideologically in significant ways, which have led to divergent growth rates for Democratic and Republican women legislators. First, the parties have become increasingly ideologically polarized.[30] Among voters and legislators alike, Republicans have become more conservative, while Democrats have become more liberal.[31] Such a polarization is significant, given that conservatism has been shown to limit women's office holding.[32]

One specific issue area where the parties' ideological polarization is particularly relevant for the partisan gap among women in elected office has been over issues relating to gender roles and gender equality, including the appropriate role of women and mothers.[33] Although the Republican Party used to offer greater support for gender equality than the Democratic Party, across the latter half of the twentieth century the two parties realigned over this set of policy issues. The Democratic Party emerged from this realignment with a greater commitment to gender equality in both the public and private spheres and with more explicit support for policies geared to help women balance career and family. This consistent support for women's advancement provides encouragement and motivation for working women thinking about a political career.

In contrast, the Republican Party emerged from the realignment with more conservative stances on women's issues and conflicting, if not unsupportive, messages about the idea of working mothers and women, as well as the need for more women in office.[34] As a result, Republican women, particularly working women, may not feel encouraged or supported to run for office within their party. In summary, this first theoretical framework posits that as a result of the parties' ideological polarization overall and realignment over women's place in particular, the

Democratic Party has become more open and welcoming to women candidates and better positioned to tap into the growing pool of qualified women candidates than the Republican Party, and further, that conservativism, now concentrated almost exclusively within the Republican Party, only constrains office holding among women within the Republican Party.

A second and perhaps less obvious theoretical framework concerns the regional realignment of the parties. Over the latter half of the twentieth century, the regional bases of the two parties underwent significant geographic shifts. Since the 1950s, Democrats have lost political power in the South, the region they used to dominate, while making gains in other regions of the country. In contrast, Republicans have made tremendous gains in the South while losing seats in other regions of the country, especially the Northeast.[35] While this regional realignment has been the focus of many political science analyses, its consequences for the representation of women in elective office has received less attention. Given research showing that some regions of the country are more welcoming to women office seekers than others,[36] the following chapters demonstrate how the regional realignment has contributed to the partisan gap among women officeholders at the state and national levels.

A third and related framework explores the ways that the intersection of race, ethnicity, gender, and partisanship has driven the emergence and growth of the partisan gap among women in elective office. Among the main drivers for the regional realignment mentioned earlier were issues relating to civil rights and racial equality.[37] The Democratic Party's evolution over the twentieth century to become the champion of civil rights, racial equality, and inclusivity resulted in exceptionally high levels of Democratic partisanship among voters of color, as well as lawmakers of color. This third framework posits that women's underrepresentation in political office, as well as the partisan gap, cannot be understood without considering these critical developments in American politics. The following chapters explore the extent to which the incorporation of Americans of color into political office holding in the decades following the passage of the Voting Rights Act of 1965 and with the racial realignment of the parties have created opportunities and constraints for women office seekers in the two parties.

A final framework focuses on the parties' distinctive cultures and their impact on the recruitment of women.[38] While political parties in the United States do not have the power to choose their nominees, they have come to play an increasingly important role in candidate recruitment and support.[39] Explicit encouragement and recruitment are particularly important when it comes to women candidates because women are more likely than men to need encouragement from others to conceive of themselves as candidates.[40] This theoretical perspective posits that the partisan gap may be the product of a stronger and more sustained commitment to recruiting women candidates by the Democratic Party compared with the Republican Party that is rooted in the distinctive and evolving cultures of the two parties.

Chapter 2 draws on the four theoretical frameworks just described to assess the emergence and growth of the partisan gap among state legislators. The chapter employs data drawn from a number of sources, most prominently the Center for American Women and Politics (CAWP) and the National Conference of State Legislatures (NCSL), to compare the current representation of Republican and Democratic women in state legislatures, broken down by state and geographic region, as well as the changing dynamics in their representation over the past several decades. Additionally, the chapter utilizes multivariate analyses to simultaneously explore the role of ideology, race, and party recruitment in explaining variations in the representation of Democratic and Republican women in state legislatures.

The empirical analyses provide support for all four theoretical frameworks. The realignment of the parties ideologically, and over the issue of women's place in particular, has impacted the respective abilities of the two parties to recruit, support, and elect women to state legislatures. As the Republican Party became more conservative, gains among Republican women state legislators stalled, while gains among Democratic women continued apace. The regional realignment of the parties also has contributed to the partisan gap among women in state legislatures. Over the past several decades, Republicans have made their biggest inroads in state legislatures in the South, the region of the country least hospitable to women's candidacies, which restrains opportunities for Republican women. Meanwhile, the Republican Party has been losing seats in the Northeast, the region historically most welcoming to women office seekers, and Republican women office seekers in particular. It is also interesting to note that the heavily conservative and Republican climate of the South has not hindered the growth of Democratic women in a parallel manner (see table 2.1). As state legislative seats have turned over and opened up across the Northeast, West, and Midwest, Democratic women have been quite strategic and successful at seizing these opportunities.

Additionally, the impressive gains among women state legislators of color, who have increased their representation in state legislatures at a faster rate than white women,[41] have benefited the Democratic Party almost exclusively.

The multivariate analyses in chapter 2 show that Republican women state legislators have faced their biggest obstacles and now have their lowest levels of representation in conservative states where Republicans dominate. In contrast, as the Democratic Party became more cohesively liberal and more committed to a gender equality agenda, it also became a more welcoming home for women office seekers. As a result of its support for women's professional achievement, the Democratic Party has effectively tapped into the growing pool of highly educated, working women to facilitate a steady increase in the representation of Democratic women as state legislators, while the Republican Party has not been able to do the same.

Chapters 3 and 4 focus on exploring the partisan gap among women in Congress. The 2018 congressional elections, with their impressive gains for Democratic women coupled with net losses for Republican women, were simply a magnified continuation of a several-decade-long dynamic. Chapter 3 draws on data from a number of sources, including CAWP, member profiles by the Congressional Research Service, and original data sets of the members of the 116th Congress and previous Congresses, to illustrate how the regional and racial realignment of the parties over the twentieth century and into the twenty-first century has played a role in widening the partisan gap among women in Congress. By charting changes in the partisan and gender composition of the Democratic and Republican delegations in the House and Congress overall over time, this chapter shows that, similar to the dynamic in state legislatures, Republican women have struggled to increase their numbers as their party developed a strong-hold in the South. This chapter also illustrates that the comparative success of women of color as candidates—their higher levels of representation among elected officials of color compared with white women's representation among white elected officials—has played a modest but consistent role behind the partisan gap in Congress. In addition, the chapter presents evidence that the Democratic Party has been more successful than the Republican Party in tapping into the growing pool of highly educated, professional women. In contrast, Republican women are heavily reliant on the state legislative pipeline to Congress, significantly more so than Democratic women or men of either party. This contributes to the partisan gap, and to the stalled progress of Republican women in particular, since their numbers in state legislatures have plateaued and in more than a quarter of states actually declined.

Chapter 4 focuses specifically on the theoretical framework relating to the distinctive cultures of the parties and how these cultures impact the ability of the national parties and their extended networks to recruit women candidates to Congress. This chapter, unlike the previous two chapters, which draw primarily on quantitative data, employs multiple qualitative methods. Chapter 4 draws on interviews with party and organizational elites, including women members of Congress, women candidates, high-level congressional staffers and campaign workers, current and former members of the parties' congressional campaign and national committees, and high-level individuals working for organizations committed to recruiting and/or supporting women's candidacies. The interviews with women candidates and members of Congress were particularly useful because these individuals were able to discuss firsthand the role the national parties played in their own campaigns, as well as the role party leaders have asked them to play in recruiting other women. Those working for nonparty organizations geared to support women candidates were able to provide informed, and in theory more objective, outsider perspectives on the work the two parties are doing in regard to women's candidacies.

An effort was made to gather a range of perspectives for this study, resulting in a total of twenty-one interviews: eleven with Republican party elites or people affiliated with groups seeking to elect Republican women; nine with Democratic party elites or people affiliated with groups seeking to elect Democratic women; and one with a high-level official working at a nonpartisan organization seeking to elect more women. The sample was a combination of purposive and snowball. Individuals with firsthand experience in recruiting candidates or running for office were contacted; those who agreed to be interviewed for this research often recommended additional individuals with whom to speak. All interviews were conducted between May and August 2014. In addition to my own interviews, I was given access to the key findings from in-depth interviews conducted by Public Opinion Strategies for Political Parity, a nonpartisan organization committed to electing more women, conducted with ten Republican Party leaders and four Republican female members of Congress during March and April 2014.

Drawing on interview data collected during earlier election cycles is useful as it provides insights into what the strategies and goals of the parties were in terms of women's recruitment, and whether these strategies have been sustained in the subsequent years and the degree to which they have impacted the actual recruitment of women in the subsequent election cycles. In particular, 2014 was a useful year to collect data because in 2013 the National Republican Congressional Committee (NRCC) created Project GROW, a program designed to draw on help from women members of Congress to recruit and support women candidates for the House of Representatives. Although the NRCC had asked women members to undertake informal efforts to recruit women in past election cycles,[42] those I interviewed emphasized that Project GROW was the first formal, institutionalized effort the NRCC has made to recruit women candidates. Project GROW was active in the 2014 and 2016 election cycles but has since disbanded, confirming fears of some Republican women elites I interviewed that this effort lacked deep, sustained commitment from the Republican Party organization.

In addition to interview data, chapter 4 draws on a range of documents from the parties as well as affiliated organizations committed to expanding the number of women in elective office. These documents provide insights into the methods the parties use to recruit candidates, as well as their rationale for wanting more women in office. I was particularly interested in comparing the public statements of the parties with the actual experiences of women candidates. Finally, this study draws on news media coverage of the parties' recruitment efforts as well as the experiences of women candidates. Particularly useful are media interviews with high-level individuals involved in recruiting candidates whom I was not able to interview myself, as well as more recent interviews with women candidates, officeholders, and those involved in candidate recruitment. The combination of qualitative methods employed in this chapter helps elucidate the approaches of the parties toward the recruitment of women candidates, both in theory and in practice.

Drawing on these sources of qualitative data, chapter 4 argues that the Democratic Party's more open and decentralized culture has allowed party elites and the party's organizational structure to more easily accommodate demands for political equality from feminists, as well as other previously marginalized groups, and to develop a much more integrated relationship with an extended network of groups committed to electing more women. In contrast, the Republican Party's hierarchical, top-down culture, which embraces individualism, rejects group-based claims, and holds a strong commitment to gender-neutral recruiting,[43] has made it very difficult for the party and its extended network to recruit women candidates. There is also a self-reinforcing dynamic at work. Women in elective office tend to be more committed than men to the idea that recruiting more women is a priority, and they also tend to have more women in their social networks, where much recruitment takes place.[44] This holds true for women in both parties. But with each passing election cycle, there are quite simply more Democratic women than Republican women in positions to carry out this recruitment work.

Many news stories have highlighted the Republican Party's problem with women, focusing their concern on the persistent gender gap in vote choice, with women typically supporting Democratic candidates over Republican candidates. Efforts have been made by the Republican Party to help its candidates, officeholders, and staffers "talk about women, women's issues, and the best ways to reach out to women voters" to try to combat the gender gap.[45] This book argues that the lack of women among Republicans in elective office is actually a much bigger and more consequential "woman problem" because it holds impacts for policy-making, claims of representation, and the viability of the party. The last chapter offers predictions regarding the future of the partisan gap among women in elective office and explores its profound consequences for American electoral politics and policy-making.

All signs indicate that the partisan gap among women in elective office, already dramatic in size, will likely grow larger. The causes of the partisan gap are not short-term or idiosyncratic but are grounded in structural forces that have reshaped the American party system over the last half century. The ideological, regional, and racial realignments that drive the partisan gap among women in elective office show no signs of reversing. In fact, the election of Republican Donald Trump as president may have exacerbated some of these trends and accelerated the growth of the partisan gap.

Additionally, the partisan gap has now taken on a self-reinforcing dynamic. Given research about the inspirational effects of women officeholders on young girls and women in the electorate,[46] it seems plausible that the much larger pool of Democratic women officeholders and leaders may encourage a wider swath of Democratic women to run for office and inspire the younger generation to become interested in politics compared with their Republican counterparts. Further, as women come to form a larger share of Democrats, the image of the Democratic Party as a welcome home for women seeking to influence policy through office holding is only reinforced. Future elections therefore seem likely to bring our nation closer to an even more pronounced gendering of the parties-in-government, which will significantly shape both the substance and the appearance of American politics. While the continued progress of women among Democratic elected officials is heartening, the concentration of women in one party is troubling. It will be nearly impossible for women to achieve proportional representation if they remain so heavily concentrated in only one party.

The last chapter also offers concrete examples of the ways Democratic women's continued growth and presence in legislatures have changed legislative agendas and policy outcomes. This chapter looks specifically at states where Democratic women now form the majority of Democratic state legislators and are in a position to control the legislative agenda. Conversely, the chapter explores the contexts in which the voices of conservative and Republican women are being distinctively undervoiced. Although Republican women, in keeping with their party's culture, are not comfortable with the idea of "women's issues" or women as a special group within the party, Republican women in elective office are in complete agreement with one another that they bring unique and important perspectives to the policy-making process.[47] The dramatic underrepresentation of Republican women in office is also a concern because the views of Republican women are distinctive from those of Republican men.[48]

Moreover, the small and in many states dwindling number of Republican women legislators limits the pool of Republican women who are well positioned to mount successful campaigns for higher-level office, including Congress, governorships, and the presidency. As the second decade of the twenty-first century comes to a close, many people, including Republicans themselves, question whether a party that remains overwhelmingly white and overwhelmingly male can effectively speak to and about women's issues.[49] In addition to these issues, the conclusion to this book offers some interesting and needed directions for future research on the partisan dynamics among women in elective office.

1

A Tale of Two Parties

The Changing Electoral Environment

Women were excluded from full citizenship and participation in politics for the majority of US history. It was not until 1920 that women received constitutional protection for the right to vote, and not until the second wave of the women's movement in the late 1960s and 1970s that the idea of having women proportionately represented in political institutions became a broadly discussed goal. Since that time, women's representation in elective office has increased, but much more slowly than many anticipated. A major reason for the surprisingly slow movement toward gender equality in all types of political office in the United States is the partisan gap among women elected officials. The trajectory of Democratic and Republican women officeholders has been strikingly different. Democratic women have made impressive strides toward proportional representation. In comparison, Republican women's progress has stalled and in some cases even reversed. The central objective of this book is to understand the dynamics behind the partisan gap among women elected officials, and thus develop a fuller understanding of why women remain underrepresented in political office in the United States and what can be done to make our political institutions more representative of all Americans.

Scholars have produced an impressive body of scholarship dedicated to understanding the reasons for women's continued underrepresentation in elective office. These studies have yielded important insights into the factors perpetuating the overrepresentation of men in elective office and acting as obstacles to women's office seeking and office holding. Much of the research on women's representation has focused on women as one cohesive group. Such a focus obscures the reality that women's representation in political office is fundamentally shaped by party and that the experiences of Republican women and Democratic women office seekers have been strikingly different. Thus, a key to understanding women's progress and obstacles is to explore women in elective office separately and comparatively across party, and to do so over time, both before and after the emergence of the partisan gap.

This chapter lays out several theoretical frameworks that act as plausible explanations for the emergence and growth of the partisan gap among women in office. Each of these frameworks identifies major shifts in the American electoral environment and party politics over the last half century and explores how these structural changes hold potential consequences for women's representation within the two parties. These frameworks include the ideological polarization of the parties in general and over issues of gender roles and gender equality in particular; the regional realignment of the parties; the incorporation of Americans of color into political office along with the realignment of the parties over issues of racial equality and inclusion; and, finally, the way that the parties' distinctive cultures shape their approaches to recruiting women candidates. While this chapter discusses each of these frameworks separately, the structural changes each of them draws our attention to are not mutually exclusive. On the contrary, all four of these structural developments in American electoral and party politics are intimately intertwined and in many cases reinforce one another.

Ideological Polarization and the Partisan Gap among Women in Elected Office

The first theoretical framework concerns party polarization in general and over issues of women's roles and gender equality in particular. One of the most profound developments in American politics over the last half century has been ideological polarization of the two major parties.[1] Well into the 1980s, at both the mass and elite levels, there were many Democrats and Republicans who identified as moderate. There were even Republican *liberals* and Democratic *conservatives* both in elected office and among everyday Americans.[2] Over the past several decades, the parties have polarized ideologically, with Republicans becoming much more conservative and Democrats becoming more liberal. As a result of this ideological realignment, both parties have become more internally cohesive and further apart ideologically.[3] It is important to note that the ideological polarization characterizing the two parties has been asymmetrical; Republicans have moved further to the right than Democrats have moved to the left.[4] Political scientists Matt Grossman and David A. Hopkins argue that the Republican Party has become, at its core, a party organized around the central motivating principle of ideological conservatism, whereas the Democratic Party views ideology as less important.[5]

The impact of this partisan polarization has been dramatic and wide-reaching, affecting everything from presidential candidate evaluations and election outcomes,[6] to what car people buy,[7] and where people live.[8] Partisan polarization also holds potential implications for women's representation. A number of studies show that state and district ideology can help or hinder women office seekers. States with more conservative and Republican electorates and more traditional cultures as defined by Daniel Elazar's typology of state political cultures tend to have fewer women in their state legislatures and congressional delegations.[9] In contrast, women have a better chance of winning elections, and are thus better represented, in states with moralistic political cultures, which emphasize political participation, as well as more liberal and Democratic electorates.[10]

Studies examining the impact of party ideology on women office seekers mostly focus on the effects of ideology on women as a single, cohesive group. Given the dramatic polarization of the parties in terms of ideology, however, it seems likely that the impact of ideology would vary dramatically by party. Given the asymmetrical polarization of the parties, the limiting impact of conservatism would work primarily to constrain opportunities for women in the Republican Party, where conservatism is now heavily if not exclusively concentrated, and thus contribute to the partisan gap among women in office.

Danielle Thomsen's theory of party fit illustrates one extension of this argument, which is that the increasingly conservative composition and reputation of the Republican Party has made Republican moderates less interested in seeking congressional office.[11] This in turn has had a constraining effect on the representation of Republican women in particular, since women have been disproportionately represented among moderate Republican elected officials. Political scientists Susan Carroll and Kira Sanbonmatsu made a similar argument focused on state legislatures, stating that: "Because Republican women legislators have been much more likely to hail from the moderate wing of the Republican Party, the increasing difficulty that moderates face in reaching office has disproportionately affected women."[12] Echoing this sentiment, former Republican US senator Olympia Snowe stated to the *New York Times,* "The Republican party's brand has veered so far right, it's not enticing for many potential women candidates to run as Republicans."[13]

Chapter 2 employs state-level measures of ideology to test the hypothesis that the dampening effect of a conservative electorate has negative effects on the representation of women within the Republican Party and has less or no impact on the fate of Democratic women office seekers. In strongly conservative states, Republican women may be less likely to view themselves as potential candidates and may receive less encouragement from others, including party leaders, to run; in addition, voters may be less likely to embrace Republican women due to assumptions that they are more liberal than their men counterparts.[14]

One particular area where the ideological polarization of the parties may have consequences for women office seekers is women's issues, and the issue of women's place in particular. For much of the twentieth century, the Democratic Party lagged behind the Republican Party in terms of its support for women's equality, but it emerged from the 1980s as the party more committed to the women's rights agenda.[15] This evolution was a response to multiple factors, including increasing ties between the Democratic Party and feminist organizations, the rise of feminists within the Democratic Party structure, and strategic calculations to reap electoral benefits from the newly emerged gender gap.[16] Over time, Democrats in elective office have become the almost exclusive actors advocating on behalf of feminist legislation, including affirmative action for women and family leave policies.[17] In its platforms and in high-profile speeches by presidents and presidential nominees, the Democratic Party came to embrace support for gender equality in all spheres, both private and public. The Democratic Party now champions policies designed to help women balance family and careers, including paid family leave and universal pre-K, and emphasizes the importance of electing more women.[18]

In contrast, since the 1970s, the Republican Party has evolved from being the party slightly more likely to advance women's rights and equality to the party less welcoming to the women's rights agenda and feminism.[19] The rising power and presence of religious-based, social conservatives among Republican Party activists, elected officials, and party leaders moved the party in a more conservative direction overall and on women's issues in particular.[20] While the Republican Party does not vilify working women and women's involvement in public office,[21] it also, not so subtly, has emphasized the desirability of more traditional roles for women and supports policies that seek to inhibit gender role change, based on the belief that women's work outside the home undermines the stability of the traditional family and the moral fabric of the nation as a whole. For example, starting in 1980, the Republican Party dropped its support for the Equal Rights Amendment and in its place began championing the vital role of homemakers. The 1992 Republican platform accuses Democrats of "forcing millions of women into the workplace" and declares that "the well-being of children is best accomplished in the environment of the home," not in childcare centers. The party also opposed policies, including the Family and Medical Leave Act and publicly funded childcare, geared to help women balance work in the public sphere with private responsibilities.[22] Across the 1990s and into the twenty-first century, congressional Republicans sponsored an increasing amount of antifeminist legislation, while moderate women within the Republican Party met with pressure to abandon any action on feminist policies.[23] The 2016 Republican platform retained an emphasis on traditional conservative family values and made no mention of paid parental leave, equal pay, or the importance of women's political leadership.[24]

The clear ideological gap between Republicans and Democrats on the issues of women's place not only characterizes the parties at the elite level but also has emerged within the general electorate, with Democrats more supportive than Republicans of policies designed to bring about gender equality in the public realm. Democrats are much more supportive than Republicans about the need for gender equality in political office. One national poll found that only 23 percent of Republicans compared with 60 percent of Democrats agreed that "it would be a good thing if more women were elected to Congress."[25] Another national poll found that when asked if having more women in public office would benefit the nation, an overwhelming 77 percent of Democrats agreed. In contrast, 62 percent of Republicans *disagreed* with the idea that having more women in office would benefit the nation.[26] These poll results reveal that at the mass level, the Democratic Party views gender equality in public office as an important goal, whereas the Republican Party has mixed if not unsupportive views regarding the idea of needing more women in office. Moreover, Republicans are much more likely than Democrats to embrace traditional views about mothers: that it is best for children if mothers do not work at all. Conversely, Democrats are more likely than Republicans to think it is good for mothers to work full-time even though it takes them away from their children.[27]

Pulling all this together, the ideological framework posits that the partisan gap among women elected officials is rooted in the ideological polarization of the parties overall and in the issue of the proper role of women in particular. As a result of the parties' ideological realignment over women's roles, the Democratic Party became better positioned than the Republican Party to attract, recruit, and support working women with political ambitions. The Democratic Party's clear commitment to equality for women in the public sphere, and its support for policies designed to help women balance career and family, create a welcoming environment for women thinking about a political career. In contrast, an ideology more supportive of traditional gender roles and hostile toward feminism has taken root in the Republican Party.[28] As a result, Republican women who work, especially mothers who work, may feel less encouraged to run for office within their party. Republican women may feel that their candidacies are not needed and perhaps not even wanted by their fellow partisans.

Given the parties' divergent messages about working women, I expect women in the two parties to take different paths to power and for the eligibility pool theory to help explain the representation of Democratic women more than Republican women. More specifically, I expect to find that one proxy for women's presence in the eligibility pool of office seekers, women's labor force participation, will be a strong predictor of women's presence among Democratic state legislators, indicating that the Democratic Party is effectively tapping into the growing pool of working women, but that labor force participation will not have a similar correlation for Republican women. Additionally, because the Democratic Party has come to support the advancement of women in education and all types of careers, particularly those historically dominated by men, I expect to find Democratic women in Congress, more than Republican women, to have higher levels of education, including advanced degrees, and to be more likely to emerge out of more traditionally male careers, such as the legal profession, that have acted as springboards for elective office.

A final hypothesis emerging from the ideological polarization framework is that Republican women will have higher levels of representation in part-time legislatures rather than full-time, professionalized legislatures. Previous research looking at women in state legislatures has found that professionalized legislatures have fewer women. Barbara Norrander and Clyde Wilcox speculate that this is because "full time legislatures attract a stronger pool of male competitors who make electoral victory more difficult."[29] However, the polarization of the parties over the issue of women's place suggests that these effects should be disproportionately or exclusively found within the Republican Party because full-time legislative work is less consistent with the Republican Party's more conservative position on the appropriate role of women.

Regional Realignment and the Partisan Gap among Women in Office

A second, related theoretical framework concerns the regional realignment of the parties. Over the second half of the twentieth century, the regional bases of the two parties have undergone shifts so large that many scholars have labeled this a partisan realignment. These regional shifts have, in turn, driven and/or reinforced the ideological polarization described in the previous section, pushing the Republican Party even further to the right and the Democratic Party toward greater and more cohesive liberalism.

The largest changes in the parties' regional bases of support have occurred in the South. For more than a century, the Democratic Party held tight control over political power in the South, so much so that the political scientist V. O. Key labeled the South a one-party region in his classic work *Southern Politics in State and Nation* (1949). Across the second half of the twentieth century, the Democrats steadily lost political power in the South, as white voters began to support Republican candidates and eventually abandoned the Democratic Party altogether. Although the southern partisan realignment stretched over decades and took longer to unfold at the state level than the national level, eventually the Republican Party came to dominate state legislatures, governorships, and congressional delegations in all southern states.[30]

One result of this was that Republicans representing southern states came to dominate the Republican Party coalition, shifting the party to the right ideologically.[31] Reflecting on the growing power of southerners, and hence conservatism, within the Republican governing coalition, political scientists Philip Klinkner and Thomas Schaller warn that this could have negative implications for the party. As they state, "Parties too narrowly based in one region, especially a region that is ideologically out of step with the rest of the country, confront the political equivalent of Gresham's law, as ideologically extreme views tend to become increasingly predominant within the party."[32]

While the Democratic Party lost political power in the South, it made inroads into other regions of the country.[33] Over the last quarter of the twentieth century, Democrats gained more and more political power across the North, especially in the Northeast. Writing in the wake of the 2006 elections, Klinkner and Schaller pointed out that Democrats have come to dominate the Northeast in the same way the Republicans had come to dominate in the South. Similar to the growing dominance of southerners within the Republican Party, the Democratic Party's loss of southern seats combined with growing power in the North and West held ideological implications, resulting in a more cohesively liberal Democratic Party.[34]

While this regional realignment of the parties has been the focus of analyses by scholars of party realignments and party polarization, its consequences for women officeholders, and the partisan gap among women officeholders in particular, have received less attention. Yet geography clearly matters to women's office seeking and representation. For many decades, the Northeast was the leader in terms of women's representation in state legislatures, in Congress, and in governorships.[35] Many argued that the culture of the Northeast was more liberal and also more moralistic, which in turn made it more open and welcoming to women office seekers.[36] Similarly, the West also has a long progressive streak in terms of women and politics, with many western states giving women the right to vote before the passage of the Nineteenth Amendment in 1920. Women have reached higher levels of representation in state legislatures, congressional delegations, and as governors in western states than in other regions.[37] In contrast, the South has long had the lowest levels of women's representation, not surprising given the traditional culture and conservative ideology that characterize most southern states.[38]

Linking the regional partisan realignment literature with the literature on how geography influences women's representation, this second framework offers another lens for understanding the emergence of the partisan gap among women officeholders. The regional realignment framework hypothesizes that the increasing strength of the Republican Party in the South, the region of the country most resistant to the emergence of women office seekers, combined with the Republican Party's loss of seats in the Northeast and the West, regions more welcoming to women seeking political office, acts to blunt, if not reverse, progress for Republican women. Conversely, as Democrats expand their power in the Northeast and the West, regions of the country that tend to be particularly open to women office seekers, the representation of women within the Democratic caucus steadily increased. In this way, the regional realignment of the parties may contribute to the emergence and growth of the partisan gap among women in elective office in state legislatures and in Congress.

The Intersection of Race, Ethnicity, Gender, and the Partisan Gap

A third theoretical framework examines how the intersection of race, ethnicity, and gender in American political development contributes to the partisan gap among women in elective office. Drawing on the theory of intersectionality pioneered by legal scholar Kimberlé

Crenshaw, this theoretical lens explores the way gender interacts with other historically marginalized identities, in particular race and ethnicity, to shape opportunities for office holding within the two parties.[39] Two critical and interrelated developments in American electoral politics inform this framework: the incorporation of Americans of color into the US political system, and the realignment of the parties over issues of race.

Incorporation into the US political system has been a slow process for Americans of color. It was not until the 1960s that African Americans and other minority groups were given a claim to political equality with the passage of the Civil Rights Act (1964) and the Voting Rights Act (1965). The passage of these laws, along with the Immigration and Nationality Act of 1965, changed the composition of the American electorate in dramatic ways, leading to significant increases in voters of color.[40] The passage of these major civil rights laws also led to significant increases in the representation of people of color in political office at both the state and the national level.[41] Particularly important in the incorporation of Americans of color into state legislatures and the US House of Representatives were the Supreme Court's series of decisions interpreting the 1965 Voting Rights Act and its extensions, and the subsequent creation of majority-minority districts after each census, particularly in the wake of the 1990 census.[42] These majority-minority districts were composed of a majority of voters of color, which helped candidates of color win elections in states characterized by racially polarized voting. Additionally, because these districts were newly formed, they did not have incumbents and therefore represented ideal opportunities for previously excluded groups to enter Congress or state legislatures.[43]

Office seekers of color made significant advancements in the wake of the Voting Rights Act. In 1965, there were no Black Americans in the US Senate and only six Black American members of the US House of Representatives. As of the 116th Congress (2019–2021), there are fifty-five Black Americans in Congress, fifty-two in the House of Representatives, and three in the Senate.[44] There has also been a marked increase in the number of Black state legislators.[45] Progress for other groups of color—the Latinx community, Asian Americans and Pacific Islanders, and Indigenous Peoples—has been slower but shows similar upward trends at the state and national levels.

When we examine the increases of Black, Latinx, Asian American, and Indigenous/Native American elected officials through an intersectional lens, looking simultaneously at race, ethnicity, and gender, we see divergent patterns for white women versus women of color. As a result of a number of structural forces, including the intersection of systemic racism and systemic sexism, women of color entered state- and national-level elective office later than white women and later than men of color. Since the late 1980s, however, women of color have increased their representation among elective officials of color in state legislatures and Congress at a faster rate than white women have among white lawmakers,[46] leading scholars to theorize that there is now a strategic advantage at the intersection of race, ethnicity, and gender for women candidates.[47] As women of all racial and ethnic backgrounds have increased their presence in the traditional candidate eligibility pool—the careers that typically lead to elective office—women of color have been particularly successful at translating these gains into greater representation in elective office.[48] Women of color have been particularly ambitious and strategic in running for newly created majority-minority districts as well as other open seats at both the state and the national level.[49] In recent elections, women of color also have been notably successful at challenging incumbents in primary elections and winning both primary and general elections despite a lack of party recruitment or support.[50] Importantly, women of color benefit from symbolic empowerment, very high levels of support from historically marginalized groups who see themselves in their candidacies and feel particularly connected to their presence on the political stage.[51] For example, a key engine behind the success of Black women candidates has been that Black women voters have turned out in high numbers and given remarkably high levels of support to Black women candidates.[52] In some cases, women of color face lower levels of perceived racial threat among voters than their men counterparts.[53] Political scientists Nadia E. Brown and Pearl K. Dowe illustrate how Black women candidates in particular are able to tap into their personal networks to overcome inconsistent support from political parties and the greater challenges they face running for office.[54]

A related issue is the partisan realignment over issues of race. The historical struggle between the African American community aiming to secure political rights and power and those seeking to block the advancements of this group has been a pivotal influence on American political development and the evolution of political parties in the United States.[55] The Republican and Democratic parties responded in very different ways to demands for civil rights and racial equality. After a century of giving voice to the cause of racial equality and issuing progressive civil rights platforms, the Republican Party changed course in 1964 and began embracing policies considerably less supportive, if not antithetical, to the civil rights agenda. Meanwhile, the Democratic Party, once the party of slavery, white supremacy, and segregation, embraced the civil rights agenda by 1964 and continued to champion the cause of racial equality and policies designed to address racial inequalities.[56]

The realignment of the parties over issues of race did not end in the twentieth century but has continued into the twenty-first century. Hetherington, Long, and Rudolph show that racial attitudes among Republicans have become increasingly conservative from the 1980s through the present, and that these conservative racial attitudes have become more powerful in explaining how Republicans evaluate candidates and view the political world.[57] Similarly, Wong demonstrates how racial anxieties, anti-immigrant sentiments, and the perception that whites face discrimination have motivated the politics of white evangelicals, a key part of the Republican Party coalition, for decades.[58] Scholars have also tracked a long-term rise among Republicans in white identity politics, wherein people find their social identification as white Americans to be important to them and predictive of their political views, as well as an embrace of white identity politics by some elites within the Republican Party.[59]

The 2016 presidential campaign and governing style of President Trump have exacerbated the racial polarization of the parties. Abramowitz and McCoy show that Trump's explicit appeals to racial and ethnic resentment helped fuel his surprising victory.[60] Hooghe and Dassonneville also show how racial resentment and anti-immigrant sentiment were powerful and equally strong predictors of voting for Republican presidential candidate Donald

Trump in 2016.[61] Similarly, Jardina shows that in the 2016 election, Trump's anti-immigrant platform capitalized on racial and ethnic animosity among Republicans.[62] Importantly, scholarship in this area underscores that partisan polarization over issues of race and ethnicity was ongoing before Trump's emergence on the national political scene, which suggests that it will likely continue after his exit from the national stage.

The ongoing realignment of the parties over racial issues has resulted in high and growing levels of Democratic partisanship among voters of color, and in turn legislators of color. In the 116th Congress, 90 percent of the Black, Indigenous, and People of Color (BIPOC) members are Democrats. Levels of Democratic partisanship among women of color in elected office are even higher. While the United States continues to become more diverse in terms of race and ethnicity, Republican officeholders at the state and national levels have become less diverse. In other words, the Republican party-in-government not only has become more male-dominated but also has become even more dominated by whites. The following chapters explore the extent to which this racial realignment of the parties at the mass and elite levels, along with the disproportionately high levels of success among women of color in obtaining elective office, have contributed to the partisan gap among women in elective office both in state legislatures and in Congress.

Distinctive Party Cultures and the Recruitment of Women Office Seekers

The fourth theoretical framework explored as a possible contributor to the partisan gap is recruitment, and more specifically the extent to which the Democratic and Republican party elites, party organizations, and their extended networks work to recruit and support women as candidates. On the one hand, the role of parties in recruiting women candidates in the United States is limited. Political parties do not have official power to select their nominees, and campaigns are notoriously candidate-centered. Yet, parties have come to play a significant and increasingly important role in recruiting and supporting candidates.[63] Elected leaders and the parties' organizations at the state and national levels have taken on an increasingly active role in encouraging particular candidates to run, especially in strategically important races, and offering select candidates a range of valuable campaign support services.[64] Party organizations doing such work are also better funded and more active than they were in the past.[65] Moreover, each of the parties benefits from an extended network of interest groups and political action committees (PACS) that work in tandem with the parties to identify and support preferred candidates for office.[66]

Explicit encouragement and recruitment are particularly important when it comes to women candidates because women are more likely than men to need encouragement from others in order to conceive of themselves as candidates.[67] Drawing on a survey of state legislators, Carroll and Sanbonmatsu found that traditional ambition theory does not adequately capture the candidate emergence process for women. Women's decision to run for office is better captured by a relationally embedded model, wherein women depend on explicit encouragement from others, especially party leaders, to spark their political ambition.[68] Speaking in January 2014, Republican senator Kelly Ayotte, who then represented New Hampshire in the US Senate, made a similar point, stating, "With all due respect to my male colleagues, a lot of them get up and they look in the mirror and they see a United States senator. Women who have accomplished so many other things in their lives don't necessarily look in the mirror and see a U.S. Senator."[69]

In her decades-long research on the relationship between parties and women's office holding, political scientist Barbara Burrell argues that while the parties, at one time, may have been a barrier to women candidates, working to recruit men over women or to recruit women for unwinnable races, this is no longer the case.[70] Both parties have launched programs specifically designed to encourage more women to run and offer specialized support for women candidates. Both parties also have extended networks of affiliated interest groups and PACs such as EMILY's List on the left and VIEW PAC and Maggie's List on the right that explicitly seek to elect more women.[71] Even though both parties express interest in recruiting women, this fourth framework posits that the parties' distinctive cultures have significantly shaped the recruitment efforts of the parties and their extended networks in a way that has helped Democratic women office seekers and hindered Republican women office seekers, therefore contributing to the partisan gap among women in elective office.

While some research on political parties offers theories that seek to explain the behavior of both parties as equivalent entities, the party culture theoretical framework, pioneered by scholar Jo Freeman and further developed by Matt Grossman and David Hopkins, views the two parties as being distinct from each other, particularly in terms of the values their members hold and the way the parties are internally structured, and in terms of their operational style.[72] Defining features of the Republican Party culture include an emphasis on individualism, a lack of openness to group-based claims, and a vehement rejection of identity policy. The Republican Party's culture is also characterized by a hierarchical structure, a top-down flow of power, and emphasis on party loyalty. In contrast, the Democratic Party has an open and decentralized culture, where power flows upward, and where group identities and group-based activism are the norm.[73]

These distinctive party cultures, in turn, may have significant consequences for efforts to recruit, mentor, and financially support women office seekers. Specifically, the party culture theoretical framework posits that the Democratic Party's decentralized culture, in which power flows upward, has allowed for the integration of demands from feminists and others pushing for greater representation for women and other historically marginalized groups, and that as a result the party and party organization elites will demonstrate cohesive and meaningful commitment to recruiting women. The distinctive nature of the Democratic Party's culture also allows the space for groups committed to electing women to operate in partnership with the party and challenge the party if needed to pursue their demands, without facing retribution or questions about their loyalty, since having groups vying for influence is normal operating procedure in the Democratic Party culture.

In contrast, the Republican Party's emphasis on individualism, party loyalty, and a top-down hierarchical structure may complicate and ultimately undermine efforts by individuals within the party or the extended networks of organizations interested in electing Republican women. Given the Republican Party's commitment to what political scientist Malliga Och has labeled "gender neutral" recruitment and disdain of identity politics, as well as the reluctance of Republicans to discuss the inherent value in electing more women,[74] a hypothesis explored in this book is that Republican efforts to recruit women will not be well supported among Republican elites and that strong party organizations will therefore correlate with fewer Republican women in state legislatures. Moreover, the Republican Party's more hierarchical structure and its emphasis on loyalty will make it difficult for the extended network of groups committed to recruiting women candidates to meaningfully interact with, let alone challenge, the party in pursuit of their goals.

Finally, I anticipate finding a reinforcing dynamic within the party cultures. Jo Freeman points out that party culture is formed in part out of the values and life experiences of its members.[75] I expect that having more women in elective office, and in particular more women in leadership positions, will in turn produce more robust recruitment of women. Although there is little systematic evidence that male party leaders in the twenty-first century are blatantly biased against female candidates, there is evidence that women are more likely than men to think recruiting women is important and to have other women in their social networks, where much recruitment takes place.[76] And there are many, many more Democratic women than Republican women in office and in leadership positions who are positioned to implement their values and do this recruiting work, and thus to shape or reaffirm their party's commitment around the value of recruiting women. I also anticipate finding that the presence of women among party leaders will correlate with more women in state legislatures, but that these effects will be more pronounced in the Democratic Party given that there are so many more Democratic women in leadership positions.

The Four Theoretical Frameworks: Reinforcing Dynamics

This chapter has outlined four theoretical frameworks for understanding the emergence and growth of the partisan gap among women in elective office. Each of these lenses is grounded in major structural changes in American electoral politics over the last half century: the parties' ideological polarization, regional realignment, and racial realignment and the ways that these forces have come to shape and reaffirm the parties' cultures. The following chapters explore these theoretical frameworks empirically in the context of state legislatures and Congress. It is important to keep in mind the ways that these structural changes are reinforcing dynamics. Indeed, the racial and regional realignments of the parties are intractably related to the parties' ideological polarization, and each of these changes has been reflected in and to some degree reinforced by the parties' distinctive cultures.

2

The Growing Chasm

Women in State Legislatures

Recent years have seen women achieving a number of historic successes in state legislatures. More women ran for state legislative seats in 2018 than ever before, and more women won. Women's representation in state legislatures grew from 25 percent to 29 percent, an increase even bigger than in the historic 1992 "Year of the Woman."[1] Nevada became the first state in US history with women as a majority of its state legislators, and Colorado emerged from the 2018 election with one of its state legislative chambers also having a majority of women.[2]

Despite these historic firsts for women's representation at the state level, women are still dramatically underrepresented, accounting for less than one-third of state legislators. Women's continued underrepresentation is troubling for those concerned about symbolic and descriptive representation. State legislatures are crucial arenas of policymaking. In recent years, states have been policy innovators on the minimum wage, health care, and criminal justice reform, as well as being on the forefront in restricting and protecting reproductive rights. As Congress remains unable to take action on most policy issues due to gridlock and partisan paralysis, states have become increasingly important centers of policy-making. Yet women remain a minority voice in debating and shaping these policies, many of which have a disproportionate and disparate impact on women. State legislatures are also well-established pipelines for higher-level political office.[3] Thus, women's continued underrepresentation in state legislatures acts as a constraint on women's office holding in Congress, in governorships, and as presidential candidates.

This chapter draws on the theoretical frameworks outlined in the previous chapter as a lens for understanding women's continued underrepresentation in state legislatures and the emergence and dynamics of the partisan gap among women legislators. The chapter begins by exploring trends in state legislative office holding among women overall, and then Democratic women and Republican women separately, paying particular attention to when the partisan gap among women state legislators emerged and the degree to which the gap coincides with the realignment of the parties ideologically and over the issues of women's place.

Next the chapter explores the representation of Republican and Democratic women in state legislatures by geographic region and by state, exploring patterns in the type of states where Democratic women and Republican women have done well, and where they have struggled to increase their representation. In particular, the chapter documents how the parties have realigned geographically in terms of state legislative seats and how these regional changes in partisan power have intersected with patterns of state legislative office holding by Democratic and Republican women. Regional power shifts are intimately related to issues of race. Therefore, the next section of the chapter explores the ways that the racial realignment of the parties combined with the overwhelming Democratic partisanship of women state legislators of color contributes to the partisan gap overall as well as in the South in particular. Finally, the chapter employs multivariate analysis to explore the factors that help and hinder the representation of Republican women compared with Democratic women, offering empirical tests of the ideological polarization, racial realignment, and recruitment frameworks.

Trends in the Representation of Democratic and Republican Women State Legislators

Women have made slow but important inroads into state legislatures. Women have increased their representation in state legislatures from 5 percent in 1971 to 29 percent as of 2020.[4] Women's representation in state legislatures steadily increased across the 1980s, but progress slowed beginning in the 1990s. Across the first two decades of the twenty-first century, from 2000 until the eve of the 2018 elections, women's representation among state legislators increased only 3 percentage points, from 22 percent to 25 percent. In some years, women's representation in state legislatures actually went down.[5] A small set of research studies have focused on explaining these trends in women's representation in state legislatures, paying particular attention to explaining why progress stalled in the 1990s and into the twenty-first century.

Paxton, Painter, and Hughes use latent growth curve models to test different theories about the trajectories of women's state legislative representation from 1982 through 2006.[6] They find that women made their biggest gains during the 1992 "Year of the Woman," even though there were no more open seats than usual in state legislative elections that year. This finding supports these researchers' gender salience hypothesis, the idea that women's representation in state legislatures increases the most when the issue of women's underrepresentation receives high-profile attention in the culture and in society. In looking at increases in representation across different decades, they find that women made the most progress entering state legislatures across the 1980s, less progress in the 1990s, and the least progress in the first decade of the twenty-first century as the nation's focus switched to terrorism. This finding is consistent with their theory that increases in women's representation are most challenging when international and national security issues, which are perceived to be masculine policy areas, dominate the national agenda.

Scholars Caroline Heldman and Lisa Wade offer a different explanation for the stagnation in women's representation in state legislatures over the first decade of the twenty-first century. They argue that "advances in communication technologies have enabled a new era of objectification, marked by an increasing presence and acceptance of sexual objectification in media, greater pornographic content in mainstream media, and greater acceptance of pornography in U.S. society more broadly."[7] This new era of objectification constrains growth among women office seekers in the twenty-first century by making it harder for voters, elites, and women themselves to take women seriously as political candidates. In other words, as objectification of women has become more pronounced and ingrained in American society, women's representation in state legislatures has stalled.

Political scientists Barbara Norrander and Clyde Wilcox also seek to explain women's stalled progress in state legislatures. They analyze change in the level of women's representation in state legislatures from 1993 to 2011 and find that the most important explanation for the slowed

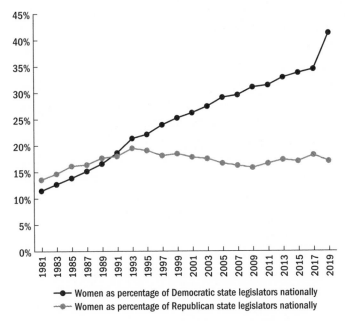

Figure 2.1. Women as a Percentage of Democratic and Republican State Legislators

progress is an increase in the proportion of seats held by Republicans. As they explain, "In states where the Republican Party gained the most seats, the number of total legislative seats held by women decreased."[8] In other words, as states became more Republican, they became less welcoming environments for women office seekers.

The studies just mentioned seek to explain the progress, or lack of progress, of women in state legislatures by focusing on women legislators as a single, cohesive group. While offering important insights, these studies obscure the fact that women's representation among Democratic and Republican state legislators has followed strikingly different trajectories. Figure 2.1 shows women as a percentage of

Democratic state legislators and women as a percentage of Republican state legislators over time.[9] The trend lines are strikingly different, with women steadily increasing among Democratic state legislators while representation for women among Republican state legislators has actually gone down. The figure vividly illustrates the extent to which research seeking to understand trends in women's representation in state legislatures as a whole misses an important reality, namely, that the dynamics of women's representation are dramatically different across the two parties.

Digging into trends in women's office holding in state legislatures by party reveals several important dynamics. The 1980s were characterized by steady growth and rough parity for women's representation within the two parties, although Republican women maintained a slight edge. Starting in the 1990s and accelerating in the twenty-first century, however, the dynamics of representation for Republican and Democratic women diverged. Women continued making strong inroads among Democratic state legislators. Year after year, decade after decade, Democratic women steadily increased their numbers and, as of summer 2020, women account for 42 percent of Democratic state legislators nationally.

In contrast, the representation of Republican women legislators hit its high point in 1993, when women represented just shy of 20 percent of Republican state legislatures. Since then, representation for Republican women has actually gone down. As of 2020, women represent only 17 percent of Republican legislators. The withering representation of Republican women since the mid-1990s is particularly surprising, since it has occurred over a period when Republicans made historic gains in state legislatures.

In 2017, Republicans held the largest number of state legislative seats at any time since 1920.[10] Yet, as Republicans seized openings and turned state legislatures from blue to red, women were not able to use these strategic opportunities to increase their presence among Republican legislators. For example, a large portion of Republican gains in state legislatures came as a result of the 2010 and 2014 elections, yet figure 2.1 shows that these two elections had little meaningful effect on women's level of representation within the Republican Party. Women came away from these Republican tidal wave elections just as marginalized among Republican state legislators as they had been previously.

What the contrasting partisan trends shown in figure 2.1 reveal is that if the heightened focus on terrorism and national security in the years after the September 11, 2001, terrorist attacks worked against women's representation in state legislatures, as Paxton, Painter, and Hughes argue, its dampening effects were felt only among Republican women.[11] Women continued to make strong inroads among Democratic state legislators in the post-9/11 years as they had during previous years and decades. Similarly, if the "new era of objectification" is undermining women's ability to be taken seriously as candidates and win state legislative races, as Heldman and Wade argue, it has been operating in that manner only for Republican women.[12]

The trends in figure 2.1 are consistent with the ideological realignment hypothesis outlined in the previous chapter. The partisan gap among women state legislators began to emerge, and women's inroads among Republican legislators stalled, as the Republican Party was shifting to the right in terms of its overall ideology as well as on issues specifically related to the appropriate role and place of women. While Norrander and Wilcox identified increased Republicanism of a state as a constraint on increases in women in state legislatures overall,[13] the trends illustrated in figure 2.1 suggest that the constraining effects of growing Republicanism have limited office-holding opportunities for Republican women only. In other words, these trends are consistent with the idea that the rightward movement of the Republican Party and its increasingly conservative ideology among both its elected officials and identifiers in the public have undermined its ability to produce, recruit, and support women state legislators.[14] Thus, either because moderate Republican women are less likely to view themselves as a good fit for their party, as Thomsen and Carroll and Sanbonmatsu argue,[15] or because increasingly conservative Republican leaders are reluctant to recruit women, starting in the 1990s and continuing through the present, the growing number of highly educated, professional Republican women are not pursuing careers in state legislatures.

Regional Realignment of the Partisan Gap among Women State Legislators

To better understand the emergence and growth of the partisan gap among women state legislators, the chapter turns now to women's representation over time, by party, across the fifty states. Geography has long held important implications for women's political incorporation and representation. The Northeast overall and the states of New England in particular were the early leaders in women's representation in state legislatures for several reasons. These states have a relatively large pool of highly educated professional women, progressive political environments, and moralistic political cultures emphasizing political participation.[16]

Western states have also had higher-than-average levels of women's representation in their state legislatures, for reasons that appear rooted in these states' long history of empowering women.[17] Many western states granted women the right to vote prior to the passage of the Nineteenth Amendment in 1920, enshrining women's franchise into the US Constitution. Additionally, many western states have weaker and more open party structures and therefore fewer obstacles that need to be overcome for women and other previously excluded groups.[18] In contrast, the South has always been and remains the region most hostile toward women office seekers. More closed party structures as well as the traditional culture prevalent in southern states have slowed women's political incorporation as both voters and officer seekers.[19]

While studies have examined the relationship between geographic regions and representation by women as a cohesive group in state legislatures, this chapter builds on those analyses by breaking women's office holding down by party and looking separately at the ways that geography has interacted with women's representation among Democratic and Republican state legislators. Table 2.1 shows the percentage of women among Republican as well as Democratic state legislators for each state, organized by geographic region—Northeast, South, West, and Midwest, employing regional classifications used by Klinkner and Schaller in their assessment of regional partisan realignments[20]—as well as the total percentage point change in women's representation within each party over three decades. This three-decade time frame allows for a comparison between a period when Republican and Democratic

TABLE 2.1. Women as a Percentage of Democrats versus Republicans in State Legislatures over Three Decades

Region/State	Percentage of Democrats Who Are Women in 2019	Percentage Change in Democrats Who Are Women from 1989 to 2019	Percentage of Republicans Who Are Women in 2019	Percentage Change in Republicans Who Are Women from 1989 to 2019
Northeast	40	+20	19	−2
Connecticut	33	+13	34	+10
Delaware	34	+30	8	−11
Maine	51	+22	21	−14
Maryland	49	+15	16	−1
Massachusetts	30	+7	18	−5
New Hampshire	47	+3	16	−13
New Jersey	38	+34	18	+5
New York	41	+23	14	+10
Pennsylvania	33	+25	21	+15
Rhode Island	40	+25	21	−6
Vermont	44	+16	29	+3
West Virginia	15	−4	14	+1
South	37	+28	13	+3
Alabama	42	+36	7	+3
Arkansas	33	+25	21	+14
Florida	45	+32	20	+3
Georgia	58	+41	12	+1
Kentucky	41	+37	12	+4
Louisiana	21	+18	14	+14
Mississippi	18	+10	11	+5
North Carolina	38	+25	15	−2
Oklahoma	48	+38	14	+10
South Carolina	22	+14	12	+2
Tennessee	26	+22	12	−4
Texas	39	+27	12	+3
Virginia	43	+35	11	+3
Midwest	45	+26	18	+1
Illinois	46	+33	16	−7
Indiana	44	+31	26	+3

Region/State	Percentage of Democrats Who Are Women in 2019	Percentage Change in Democrats Who Are Women from 1989 to 2019	Percentage of Republicans Who Are Women in 2019	Percentage Change in Republicans Who Are Women from 1989 to 2019
Iowa	45	+31	17	+2
Kansas	45	+26	20	−4
Michigan	49	+37	25	+12
Minnesota	42	+22	20	+2
Missouri	44	+26	17	+4
North Dakota	48	+36	16	+3
Ohio	49	+38	14	+6
South Dakota	38	+27	21	+9
Wisconsin	49	+32	14	−13
West	47	+24	22	+2
Alaska	27	+22	47	+23
Arizona	50	+42	29	−2
California	36	+27	17	−2
Colorado	63	+53	23	−6
Hawaii	30	+18	50	−6
Idaho	52	+42	26	+3
Montana	52	+33	15	+7
Nevada	64	+56	29	+13
New Mexico	42	+35	23	+6
Oregon	52	+41	21	+6
Utah	70	+65	11	+2
Washington	51	+27	29	+4
Wyoming	42	+32	12	−6

Notes: Statistics combine data on lower and upper chambers and are calculated by author using data from the Center for American Women and Politics, *The Book of the States*, and the National Conference of State Legislatures.

women were at rough parity with one another in terms of representation and a period in which the dynamics of women's representation across party differ dramatically. Table 2.1 allows us to identify which states and which regions of the country appear more or less hospitable to gains by Democratic women and Republican women separately, and to assess how the regional realignment of the parties has interacted with women's representation among state legislators within the two parties.

Before exploring the ways that the regional realignment of the parties intersects with women's representation over time, it is useful to compare women's representation across states, by party today. In other words, how well represented are women among Republican versus Democratic state legislators in each of the states? One reason it is important to look at women's representation by party is that scholars studying representation have argued that for women to make a meaningful impact within an institution, to move beyond token status and actually impact the agenda and operations, their representation needs to exceed a critical mass or a certain threshold percentage.[21] While the concept of critical mass is a contested one, with scholars pointing out that there is no magical proportion women must achieve in order to have a substantive effect on political decision-making and outcomes,[22] most agree that movement toward the proportional representation of women in legislative bodies is an important goal, both because equal representation is normatively important in a democracy and because it alters the deliberative processes, priorities, and outcomes of political institutions.[23]

Given all this, many responded with excitement and anticipation when Nevada became the first state with a majority of women in its state legislature in 2019.[24] Having a major political institution, such as a state legislature, run by a majority of women is an important, historic achievement. Given the decline in bipartisan cooperation and the increasingly distinct views of Republican and Democratic women in the electorate and as state legislators,[25] however, women's representation within their respective party caucuses is arguably a more meaningful indicator of women's influence than women's overall level of representation in a state legislature. The information in table 2.1 indicates that Democratic women are much better positioned than Republican women to play a meaningful role in shaping the legislative priorities, deliberations, and policy outcomes in state legislatures across the country.

Table 2.1 offers some sobering statistics about Republican women in state legislatures. Put simply, women are not well represented among Republican legislators in most states. There are only three states in which women form more than 30 percent of Republican legislators—Connecticut, Alaska, and Hawaii—and two of these states, Hawaii and Connecticut, are overwhelmingly Democratic and therefore the influence of Republicans, whether women or men, in shaping policy in these states is minimal. In fact, the cases of Hawaii and Connecticut seem consistent with research suggesting that Republican women have the best opportunities to gain power in states where political positions are seen as less valuable.[26]

The cases of Hawaii and Connecticut illustrate a broader pattern in the representation of Republican women in state legislatures. Women's representation among Republican state legislators is, on average, significantly higher in states where Democrats dominate than in states where Republicans are in control. Women represent 23 percent of Republicans in states where Democrats control the state legislature and the governorship versus only 17 percent of Republicans in states where Republicans are in control. In other words, Republican women have, on average, higher levels of representation in states where they and their Republican colleagues have little, if any, meaningful opportunity to impact the legislative agenda, deliberations, and outcomes. Another way to frame this finding is that Republican men not only are significantly overrepresented among Republican state legislators but also are especially overrepresented in states where their party rules.

Alaska is an interesting exception to this pattern. Women form 47 percent of Republican legislators in Alaska. This is a particularly meaningful accomplishment because Republicans control both houses of the state legislature. Additionally, women hold two important leadership positions in the Alaska legislature: senate majority leader and senate president.[27] Thus, Republican women are in a strong position to shape legislative priorities, deliberations, and policy outcomes in Alaska. In contrast, women only form about 27 percent of Democrats in the Alaska state legislature, which is considerably less than Democratic women state legislators' level of representation nationally as shown in figure 2.1. The strong performance of Republican women in Alaska is also not shared by other states that have an individualistic culture similar to Alaska's.[28] One factor that may help explain the strong performance of Republican women in Alaska is that while it is a red state with a Republican-controlled state legislature, a Republican governor, and two Republican senators, it is one of the least conservative red states in terms of state ideology.[29] Second, the early success of Republican women in high-profile elective offices in Alaska—Lisa Murkowski becoming one of the state's US senators in 2002 and Sarah Palin becoming the governor in 2006—may have helped pave the way for Republican women in the state legislature by normalizing the idea of women's power within Alaska's Republican Party and encouraging more conservative women to consider candidacies.

In contrast to their Republican counterparts, women form 30 percent or more of Democrats in the vast majority of states, forty-four of the forty-nine listed in table 2.1 (Nebraska is not included because it has a nonpartisan legislature). In fact, women form 40 percent or more of Democratic state legislators in thirty-two states. Most strikingly, women now form 50 percent or more of Democratic legislators in ten states: Arizona, Colorado, Idaho, Georgia, Maine, Montana, Nevada, Oregon, Washington, and Utah. The historic achievements of women in the state legislatures of Colorado and Nevada, mentioned previously, are in fact driven by Democratic women; women form 63 percent of Democratic legislators in Colorado and 64 percent of Democratic legislators in Nevada. Democratic women's high levels of representation in Nevada and Colorado are all the more meaningful because their party holds the majority, and Democratic women hold leadership positions in both of these states.[30] Moreover, in contrast with their Republican counterparts, women's representation among Democratic legislators is slightly (3 percentage points) higher in states where Democrats are in control than in states where Republicans are in control. The broader significance is that women are well positioned to shape the Democratic Party's policy agenda and strategy in most state legislatures, particularly in those states controlled by Democrats.

As discussed in the preceding chapter, the parties have realigned geographically over the past half century, a trend that has shaped the partisan dynamics of legislative office holding at both the state and national levels. Overall partisan shifts in state legislative office holding over the three-decade period focused on in table 2.1 reflect these broader dynamics.

One important partisan dynamic in state legislatures has been an overall increase in power for Republicans. The 2018 elections were not good for Republicans, resulting in a loss of state legislative seats for Republicans overall and Republican women in particular. Yet, in the three decades prior, Republicans made historic gains. Republicans emerged from the 2016 elections in control of sixty-seven state legislative chambers, the most the party has held throughout its history, as well as more than 4,160 state legislative seats, the most Republicans have held since 1920.[31] Republicans also emerged from the 2016 elections with thirty-three governorships, more than at any time since 1922. Over the thirty-year time frame highlighted in table 2.1, Republicans increased the number of state legislative seats under their control by 917. Republicans now hold 52 percent of state legislative seats.[32]

In terms of regional dynamics, the biggest partisan shifts in state legislative seats have occurred in the South. Partisan realignment in state legislatures in the South occurred later than the realignment in the South at the presidential and congressional levels. Even as late as 1993, Democrats held more than two-thirds of state legislative seats in Alabama, Georgia, Louisiana, North Carolina, and Oklahoma.[33] Thus, the three-decade period highlighted in table 2.1 shows the dynamics of the partisan gap in the South from a time when Democrats still dominated southern legislatures to a time when Republicans maintain a large political advantage in the region. In 1989, Democrats held 64 percent of state legislative seats in the South. Moreover, at that time, Democrats held more seats in the South, by far, than in any other region of the country.

The concentration of Democratic strength in the South throughout the 1980s appears to have been a factor constraining the representation of Democratic women state legislators. The greatest opportunities for Democratic office holding for many decades were in southern states, which were dominated by a traditional culture and conservative views on women's place.[34] Given that, it is not surprising that as of 1989, women formed only 9 percent of Democratic legislators in southern states, which was lower than their level of representation in any other region.

As the Democratic Party lost power in the South, it made gains in other regions of the country, especially the Northeast and to a lesser degree the West. Both of these regions are characterized by political cultures friendly to women office seekers. As seats in the Northeast and the West flipped from red to blue, Democratic women had opportunities to make inroads in fairly welcoming political environments. Over the course of three decades, women increased their presence among Democrats in state legislatures in the West by 24 percentage points, and they increased their presence among Democratic state legislators in the Northeast by 20 percentage points. Currently, women form 47 percent of western Democrats and 40 percent of Democrats in northeastern state legislatures. In other words, as a result of their party's shifting geographic bases, women in the Democratic Party went from facing a tough and unwelcoming political and cultural environment in the South to facing much more favorable political environments in other regions of the country.

The pattern for the Republican Party follows the opposite trajectory as the one just described. In 1989, Republicans held only 36 percent of state legislative seats in the South. The South was the region where the Republican Party held the fewest seats. But by 2019, a dramatic shift had occurred. In the wake of the 2018 elections,

Republicans held 64 percent of state legislative seats in the South, higher than the percentage of seats they held in any other region. Over the last three decades, therefore, the best and most numerous opportunities for Republican gains have been in the South. Moreover, the South has become the regional power base of the Republican Party, a situation that has implications for the party's reputation and ideology overall.[35]

The Republican Party's growing strength in the South has had clear consequences for women office seekers in the party. As the regional realignment unfolded, the electoral landscape for Republican women became more, not less, challenging. The best opportunities for Republicans seeking state legislative office over the past several decades, either to flip seats from Democrat to Republican or to run in safe Republican seats that open up, have been in the South, the region most resistant to women in office. The fact that the best opportunities to gain legislative seats have been in the conservative, traditional climate of southern states helps explain why women's representation among Republican state legislatures has actually decreased by 1 percentage point over the past three decades. As table 2.1 shows, even though Republican women face challenges in all regions, they clearly face their biggest roadblocks in the South, where women form only 13 percent of Republican state legislators. Given the fact that the majority of women in many southern states vote for Republican candidates and identify as conservatives, the problem is not a lack of Republican women as potential state legislative candidates. The pronounced underrepresentation of Republican women in southern states is particularly concerning because the South has become the power center of the Republican Party and represents one of the party's leading areas of opportunity for higher office and leadership.

Although not as dramatic as the southern realignment, partisan change also occurred in the Northeast. Over the three-decade period highlighted in table 2.1, Republicans lost 122 seats in the Northeast, going from holding 947 to 825 legislative seats. This too has had consequences for women in the Republican Party. The Northeast was the early leader in terms of women's representation in state legislatures.[36] Thus, as the Republican Party lost ground in the Northeast, it lost out on opportunities in the region most hospitable historically to women office seekers. Table 2.1 shows that the partisan realignment in the Northeast has been disproportionately harmful to women in the Republican Party. As of 2019, women form 19 percent of Republican state legislators in the Northeast, which is 2 percentage points lower than their representation in 1989. The decline in representation among Republican women has been particularly pronounced in the states of New England.[37] The decline of Republican women in the Northeast overall and New England in particular is consistent with the ideological polarization framework and the idea that the growing conservatism of the party has made legislative office particularly unwelcoming to moderate Republican women, since the Northeast and New England in particular have traditionally been a home for moderate Republicans.

What is also interesting is that Democratic women not only have been able to make gains in the Northeast and the West, two regions historically more open to women office seekers and where the Democratic Party has made gains, but have also made striking gains in the Midwest and the South, regions of the country where Democrats overall have lost power. The gains among Democratic women in the South are particularly striking. Even though Democrats have suffered huge losses in southern legislatures over the last three decades, women have nevertheless made strong inroads among southern Democratic legislators, increasing their presence from 9 percent to 37 percent. In six southern states, women now form more than 40 percent of Democratic legislators. In other words, as of today the traditional and conservative culture of the South is holding back only Republican women.

The progress of Democratic women shows that geography is no longer holding Democratic women back from making steady inroads into state legislatures. Republican women are clearly confronting obstacles in the South, but Democratic women are making gains in all regions of the country. Three intersecting developments are behind these contrasting dynamics. One is that the conservatism and traditional attitudes about women's place that have long characterized southern culture are now, as a result of ideological realignment and polarization, concentrated among Republicans at the mass and elite levels and thus are constraining only Republican women. The Democratic Party may also be engaging in more effective recruitment of women than the Republican Party, and the large number of well-educated, well-qualified Republican women in southern states are simply not being asked or encouraged to run. These ideas are explored in more detail later in this chapter. Finally, the strong performance of women of color combined with their overwhelming Democratic partisanship appears to be a factor behind the divergent performance of Democratic and Republican women legislators overall, but particularly in the South. The chapter now turns to explore this last factor in more detail.

Racial Realignment and the Partisan Gap in State Legislatures

A factor closely related to regional realignment in state legislatures is the racial realignment of the parties. Drawing on the intersectional framework discussed previously, this chapter now considers the role of race and ethnicity in shaping the partisan gap among women in state legislatures. After facing both formal and informal exclusion from political office holding, Americans of color have slowly increased their representation in state legislatures in the wake of the 1965 Voting Rights Act. In 1972, roughly 97 percent of state legislators across the country were white men, and about 2 percent were Black men.[38] Today, Black Americans form more than 9 percent of state legislators. Gains among other groups of color, including Latinx and Asian Americans, have lagged behind those of Black Americans but show similar upward trends.[39]

The passage of the 1965 Voting Rights Act and the subsequent creation and expansion of majority-minority districts, defined as districts where non-Hispanic whites form a minority of voters, in state legislatures has been one of the most important factors behind increases in state legislators of color, especially for Black and to a lesser extent Latinx Americans.[40] Each redistricting cycle since the 1970s has led to an increase in the number of majority-minority districts and in turn the number of Americans of color as state legislators.[41] The size of the Black, Latinx, or Asian American community within a state is the single biggest predictor of the representation of Americans of color in state legislative office.[42] Black Americans have made their biggest gains in legislatures in southern states, where they form the largest share of the population.[43]

Meanwhile, Latinx Americans and Asian Americans have made their biggest inroads in state legislatures in the West and, in the case of Asian Americans, in California and Hawaii in particular, states where there are large communities of Latinx and Asian American voters.

Given the intersection of racism and sexism in American politics, women of color entered state legislative office after white women and men of color.[44] Despite this later start, as well as the distinct and steeper challenges women of color face as state legislative candidates,[45] women of color increased their presence in state legislatures at a faster rate than white women. The comparative success among women legislators of color is driven in part by strategic decisions on the part of women of color to run for open seats and in part by high levels of support their candidacies have received from historically marginalized communities empowered by the presence of someone who looks like them seeking electoral office: voters of color, women voters, and, at the intersection of the two identities, women voters of color, which political scientist Evelyn Simien labels symbolic empowerment.[46] As a result, even though women of color, and people of color more broadly, remain underrepresented in state legislatures relative to their presence in the population, women of color are actually better represented among state legislators of color than white women are among state legislators who are white. In 2010, white women formed 22.8 percent of white state legislators. In comparison, Black women formed 38.4 percent of Black legislators, Latinx women formed 31.6 percent of Latinx lawmakers, and Asian American women formed 36.6 percent of Asian American legislators.[47] The relative overrepresentation of women of color compared with white women has continued through to the present and holds significant implications for the partisan gap because of the disproportionately Democratic partisanship among state legislative women of color.

As a result of the racial realignment of the political parties, legislators of color are an overwhelmingly Democratic group.[48] Indeed, in nine southern states, including the five deep southern states of Alabama, Georgia, Louisiana, Mississippi, and South Carolina, Black Americans form the majority of Democratic state legislators, while the Republican state legislators in those states are almost entirely composed of white Americans.[49] Americans of color combined also compose the majority of Democratic state legislators in Arizona, California, and Nevada. In New Mexico, the majority of Democratic state legislators are Hispanic.[50] The overwhelming Democratic partisanship of state legislators of color is continuing to grow even more pronounced with each election cycle. For example, the 2018 election resulted in an increase in the number of Democratic state legislators of color and a decrease in the number of Republican state legislators of color.[51]

Democratic partisanship is even more pronounced among women state legislators of color. Currently, 25 percent of women in state legislatures are women of color; an overwhelming 97 percent of these women are Democrats. Black women state legislators are the most Democratic group, with 99 percent identifying as Democrats.[52] Thus, a significant driver for the strong performance of Democratic women in state legislatures and the growth and emergence of the partisan gap has been the incorporation of women of color into state legislative office holding. As more women of color have been elected to state legislatures, the partisan gap among women in elective office has grown. If women of color were represented in state legislatures at the same lower levels as white women, there would be significantly fewer Democratic women in state legislatures. While the partisan gap would not disappear, it would be meaningfully smaller.

Indeed, the relationship between gender, race, and partisanship helps explain the somewhat surprising partisan gap in southern legislatures in particular. The previous section noted that Democratic women have made inroads into southern legislatures, which to some degree was unexpected given the South's traditional culture and conservatism. A key reason for the strong performance of Democratic women in the South has been the high success rates of Black women as state legislative candidates. In most state legislatures in the South, Black women are now the majority of Democratic women legislators.[53] In Alabama, for example, all of the Democratic women in the state legislature are Black. This helps explain why Alabama has one of the largest partisan gaps among all of the states, with women forming 42 percent of Democratic legislators but only 7 percent of Republican legislators. Along similar lines, Black women also form 92 percent of Democratic women legislators in Mississippi, 82 percent in Louisiana, 75 percent in Tennessee, 71 percent in South Carolina, and 65 percent in Georgia.[54] Once again, the strong performance of Black women is a driving reason that Georgia has the largest partisan gap of all the states, wherein women compose a stunning 58 percent of Democratic legislators compared with just 12 percent of Republican legislators. Without the strong performance of Black women, Democratic women would have little representation in southern legislatures. That said, it is also important to note that while Black women have achieved impressive levels of representation among Democratic legislators in southern states, their influence is significantly curtailed by the fact that the Republican Party maintains control over state legislatures and governorships in all southern states.[55]

While majority-minority districts and strong support from voters of color have been important drivers behind the increased representation of women of color in state legislatures, and hence the partisan gap among women state legislators, multiple studies suggest that the representation of women of color, as well as Americans of color more broadly, is not tied solely to majority-minority districts or support from voters of color. While, at one point in history, heavily Black districts may have been necessary to overcome racially polarized voting and allow Black voters to elect a preferred candidate to office, recent research finds that this is no longer the case.[56] Black candidates have been succeeding in districts where white voters are the majority. This is also the case for Latinx candidates.[57] This is important not only in terms of future advances for state legislators of color but also in light of the Supreme Court's decision in Shelby v. Holder (2013), which ended the federal government's role in preapproving redistricting plans to ensure they are not disadvantaging communities of color.

In the end, the racial realignment of the parties along with the greater success of women of color in achieving state legislative office compared with white women cannot explain all of the partisan gap. Indeed, the partisan gap among women state legislators exists, and is quite pronounced, even in the very white states of Maine, Vermont, and Wyoming. Yet, the evolving intersection of race/ethnicity, gender, and partisanship in American electoral politics meaningfully contributes to the partisan gap among women in state legislative office and is a significant driver of Democratic women's ability to attain robust levels of representation in the South.

Predictors of Women's Representation by Party: A Multivariate Analysis

The final section of this chapter employs multivariate analysis to further explore the role of the theoretical frameworks discussed in chapter 1 and better understand the factors that help or hinder the representation of Democratic versus Republican women in state legislatures. Table 2.2 presents the results of OLS multivariate regression analysis predicting the percentage of women among Democratic and Republican legislators, combining both lower and upper houses, across the states. The representation of women within the two parties is modeled as a function of factors expected to help or hinder women's success differentially based on party including state ideology, women's presence in the candidate eligibility pool, whether the state has a full-time/professional legislature, whether a state has multimember state legislative districts, party organizational strength, whether the state has term limits, and whether there was a woman in a position of leadership in the state in the prior legislative term. Since the ideological, racial, and party culture/recruitment frameworks posit that these factors will differentially affect the success of women within the Republican and Democratic parties, I estimate the models separately by party.

The ideological polarization framework offers three hypotheses related to the partisan gap among women in state legislative office that are tested in the multivariate models. First, as a result of the ideological polarization of the parties, conservatism, which has been shown to predict fewer women in political office, will work to undermine the representation of women only in the Republican Party, where conservatism is now concentrated. The second hypothesis emerging from the ideological polarization framework is that due to the parties' realignment and polarization over women's place, the eligibility pool will be a more effective pipeline for Democratic women than Republican women. The third hypothesis is that Republican women may do comparatively poorer in highly professional legislatures than in part-time legislatures, because full-time legislative work is less consistent with the Republican Party's more conservative position on the appropriate role of women.

Table 2.2 shows support for two of these three hypotheses. The first hypothesis relates to state ideology. The measure for state ideology has been coded on a scale of 0 to 1, so that higher scores indicate a more conservative state electorate.[58] As predicted, conservatism of a state is a strong and robust predictor of fewer women among Republican legislators. One might presume that more conservative states would offer a relatively more welcoming environment for Republican candidates—and indeed they do—but only for Republican men. Republican women actually have lower levels of representation among their party's legislators in more conservative states.

The strong relationship between greater conservatism in a state and fewer women among Republican legislators is consistent with the ideological polarization framework. It suggests that the increasingly conservative ideology that has come to define the Republican Party at the elite and mass levels as well as the overall culture of the party have created a formidable barrier for Republican women office seekers. Whether Republican women in highly

TABLE 2.2. Predictors of Women among Democrats and Republicans in State Legislatures, 2019

	Percentage Women among Democratic Legislators	Percentage Women among Republican Legislators
Ideological Realignment Theory		
Conservatism of state electorate	.159 (.115)	−.223 (.081)***
Percentage women in workforce	.862** (.438)	−.001 (.306)
Professional legislature	−.046 (.040)	.045 (.029)
Racial Realignment		
Multimember districts	−.019 (.040)	.057** (.028)
Party Culture and Recruitment		
Republican woman leader		.030 (.022)
Democratic woman leader	.070** (.033)	
Party organization strength	−.003 (.010)	−.016** (.007)
Term limits	.067* (.036)	.017 (.025)
Constant	−.319 (.348)	.292 (.247)
Observations	49	49
R-squared	.290	.363

Note: Cell entries are unstandardized coefficients; standard errors in parentheses.
*p < .1
**p < .05.
***p < .01 two-tailed tests.

conservative states do not feel welcome running for office in a party that is ambivalent about the role of working women and the need for more women in office, or they feel they are not the right fit for their party, the reality is that high levels of conservatism work against the representation of Republican women.

Conversely, the statistically significant and negative coefficient for citizen ideology in the Republican model also indicates that Republican women state legislators have their highest levels of representation in states that are more liberal. Almost by definition this means that the seats of Republican women are distinctively vulnerable. This may help explain why the number of Republican women in state legislatures has plateaued and declined, and why Republican women have been harder hit than their male colleagues by recent Republican losses in state legislatures. In the 2018 election, for example, the number of Republican women state legislators declined at an even steeper rate proportionately than the number of Republican men. Additionally, this means that Republican women have their highest levels of representation in liberal-oriented states where opportunities for Republican advancement to statewide office, such as governorships or US Senate seats, are more challenging.

In contrast, the citizen ideology variable is not statistically significant in the Democratic women model. This indicates that the representation of women among Democratic state legislators no longer hinges on having a particular ideology among a state's citizens. Democratic women are succeeding equally well in both conservative and liberal states. This nonfinding helps explain why Democratic women have been able to post impressive gains in state legislatures in the notoriously conservative South, as well as in more liberal regions of the country such as the Northeast.

Another well-established factor influencing the representation of women in state legislatures is the number of women in the eligibility pool for state legislative office— the jobs that have traditionally led to political careers.

Following a number of other studies examining women's representation in state legislatures,[59] women's presence in the eligibility pool is operationalized as the percentage of women in the workforce in each state, as of 2016, as provided by the US Bureau of Labor Statistics. In comparison to several decades ago, the majority of women, including mothers, are now in the workforce full-time, which provides them with the resources, networks, and experiences that are typically prerequisites of political careers.[60] There is, however, wide variation in the percentage of working women across the states, ranging from a low of 63 percent in West Virginia to a high of 81 percent in Minnesota.[61]

The ideological polarization framework predicts that as a result of the partisan realignment over the appropriate role for women, Republican women who are in the workforce may not feel encouraged to run for office given their party's conflicted views on working women and its homage to traditional roles for women. In contrast, the Democratic Party's embrace of policies to aid working women and mothers, as well as the goal of gender equality in public office, should create a favorable environment for working women interested in political careers. Table 2.2 shows that, as hypothesized, women's presence in the eligibility pool significantly predicts greater representation for Democratic women, but not for Republican women. In other words, the pipeline and social networking effects of being in the workforce are operating in a positive way only for women within the Democratic Party. These results are consistent with the hypothesis that the Democratic Party has become a more effective and welcoming party for working women who are interested in political careers.

Previous research has also found that women have comparatively lower levels of representation in state legislatures with full-time, highly paid professional legislatures.[62] Barbara Norrander and Clyde Wilcox speculate that this is because "full time legislatures attract a stronger pool of male competitors who make electoral victory more difficult."[63] The ideological polarization framework posits that the exclusionary effects of professional legislatures should work to constrain Republican women more than Democratic women because full-time legislative work is less consistent with the Republican Party's more conservative position on the appropriate role of women. In the multivariate models in table 2.2, the type of legislature each state has is operationalized using data and coding from the National Conference of State Legislatures, which categorized states based on the time legislators spend on the job, their compensation, and the size of their staff. States are scored 1 if the state has a professional legislature and otherwise are scored 0. The professional legislature variable is not significant in either model, suggesting that professional legislatures no longer act as a constraint on legislative office holding for either Democratic or Republican women.

The racial realignment framework demonstrated that the incorporation of women of color into political office, and state legislatures in particular, along with their overwhelming Democratic partisanship, meaningfully contributes to the partisan gap among women in elective office. Studies of legislative office holding, however, have shown that factors that predict greater representation for white women and women of color are not the same.[64] For decades, studies have found that women's representation in state legislatures is higher in states that have multimember districts, wherein voters select multiple rather than one candidate to represent them.[65] Scholars have speculated that this effect may be because women may feel more comfortable running in multimember districts because they are part of a group and/or that voters may seek gender balance when they have the opportunity to cast a ballot for multiple candidates.[66]

Yet, at the same time, multimember districts actually work to the disadvantage of candidates of color, which is one of the major reasons fewer states have multimember legislative districts today than in the past.[67] Given the strong relationship between state legislators of color and the Democratic Party, the racial realignment framework leads to the prediction that having multimember districts will work to advance the representation of Republican women, who are overwhelmingly white, and either have no effect or will work against Democratic women, among whom women of color are well represented.

The results in table 2.2 support this extension of the racial realignment hypothesis to some degree. Having multimember districts in a state is a significant predictor of more women among Republicans state legislators, as predicted, and does not have significant effects in the Democratic model.[68] Over the years, more and more states have stopped using multimember districts, which is yet another way that the electoral environment has become more challenging for Republican women, while becoming more conducive to the diverse group of Democratic women seeking political office. The challenging nature of single-member districts for Republican women may be exacerbated in future election cycles as remaining states drop their multimember districts. For example, West Virginia has voted to drop its use of multimember districts after the 2020 census.[69]

The final theoretical framework guiding the exploration of the partisan gap among women in office concerns party recruitment. Past scholarship has shown women's representation is significantly impacted by the existence of elites who encourage or discourage women to run. Although parties in the United States do not have the power to select their candidates, the recruitment efforts of parties and affiliated groups significantly shape the decision to run, especially for women.[70] In her research on state legislatures, Kira Sanbonmatsu found that stronger party organizations had a negative effect on the representation of women among legislative candidacies and the representation of women within both parties in the lower house of state legislatures from 1971 to 1999.[71] Conversely, scholars have argued that the weaker and more open party organizations in western states have helped to account for women's higher-than-average level of representation in that region.[72]

The party culture/recruitment framework posits that as a result of their distinctive party cultures, the Democratic Party has become more effective than the Republican Party at recruiting women at both the state and the national level. Three variables are included in the models to capture aspects of this framework: a measure of party organization strength, the presence of women in state legislative leadership posts, and the presence of term limits.

As discussed in the previous chapter, differences in party organizational structure have resulted in a Democratic Party culture that is unified around the idea that having more women, and more diversity, in elective office is a good thing and welcomes targeted efforts to recruit women. In contrast, the Republican Party's hierarchical structure and focus on individualism and ideological purity have resulted in a party culture that sees gender as irrelevant to party recruitment, which in turn can work against the emergence of women's candidacies, since women rely more than men on party recruitment and encouragement from party leaders to conceptualize themselves as candidates. Carroll and Sanbonmatsu's study of state legislators and party officials found that the Republican Party overall and Republican men in particular exhibit "low levels of commitment to remedying existing gender inequalities" and see no need to make explicit efforts to recruit women.[73] They found that a sizable portion of Republican elected officials, particularly male elected officials, expressed skepticism if not hostility toward demands for gender equality within the party. One hypothesis emerging from these contrasting party cultures is that a strong party organization should help increase the representation of Democratic women but may hinder representation for Republican women.

Table 2.2 shows that this hypothesis is partially supported. Party organizational strength is statistically significant and negative in the Republican model,[74] indicating that women have lower levels of representation among Republican legislators in states with strong party organizations. This suggests that the Republican Party's "gender-neutral" recruitment philosophy may actually be working to harm women's representation. In contrast, while stronger party organization used to act as a barrier for Democratic women in state legislatures,[75] table 2.2 indicates that the strength of party organizations no longer has a significant impact, positive or negative, on women's level of representation among Democratic state legislators. The good news is that strong party organizations are not working against Democratic women; however, these null results also indicate that strong party organizations are not working to meaningfully increase women's representation either. Indeed, this null finding is consistent with the interview-based research conducted by Brown and Dowe, who found that the Democratic Party is at best inconsistent in its support of Black women candidates for local- and state-level offices, despite the crucial role Black women play as voters, candidates, and elected officials within the Democratic Party coalition.[76]

Another party culture and recruitment-related hypothesis is that the presence of women in state legislative leadership should predict more women in the legislature overall. Legislative leaders not only have power to shape priorities and policy substance but also play important roles in recruiting legislative candidates.[77] Studies suggest that men are less likely to recruit women—not because they are blatantly biased against women's candidacies, but because they have fewer women in their social networks and are inclined to recruit people like themselves.[78] Women, in contrast, are more likely to think recruiting women is important, have women in their social networks, and reach out to these women as potential candidates. Thus, the presence of at least one woman among either party's state legislative leadership in the prior term, as documented by the National Conference of State Legislatures, should be associated with a greater number of women legislators.

Table 2.2 shows that the presence of a Democratic woman in state legislative leadership does predict more Democratic women in state legislatures, but there is no parallel effect for Republican women. These contrasting results are likely driven in part by the fact that there are more Democratic women in state legislative leadership positions. Prior to the 2018 elections, there were forty-two Democratic women in state legislative leadership positions across twenty-five states versus only twenty-three Republican women across twenty states,[79] which means a much greater opportunity for Democratic women leaders to recruit other women candidates. Additionally, the positive effect of Democratic women leaders, but not Republican women leaders, is reflective of the different cultures of the two parties, wherein Democrats are open about their desire to recruit more women candidates, whereas Republicans tend to stand fast behind the idea that they do not explicitly recruit women or any particular group, but let the best candidates find the party.[80]

Finally, the model includes a measure of whether or not the state has had term limits in effect in recent years.[81] Incumbency has long been identified as one of the biggest barriers to women, or any previously excluded group, entering political office. Thus, many gender and politics scholars expected that the implementation of term limits by many states across the 1990s would create opportunities for women's advancement. Empirical explorations of the issue have produced mixed results, indicating that an increased number of open seats in and of itself will not necessarily lead to more women.[82] Without a sustained and concerted effort to encourage more women to run for the open seats, term limits do not automatically result in greater numbers of women in legislatures and can even lead to a reduction in the number of women in office as women are term limited out.

The party culture and recruitment framework posits that term limits will predict greater representation among Democratic women since there is a strong recruitment machinery to encourage them to seize these openings, but they will will not have a parallel effect on Republican women. Supporting this idea, Valerie O'Regan and Stephen J. Stambough's cross-sectional analysis from 1990 to 2014 found that term limits benefit the representation of Democratic women, but not Republican women.[83] The results in table 2.2 lend further support to this hypothesis. The presence of term limits significantly predicts more women among Democratic legislators while having no effects on Republican women. These findings are consistent with the idea that Democratic women, supported by their party and a network of affiliated women's organizations committed to the goal of gender equality in political office, are better positioned to take advantage of the openings created by term limits than their Republican counterparts. Although many of the growing number of campaign training programs for women candidates are nonpartisan, they appear disproportionately effective at helping Democratic women obtain state legislative office.[84]

Looking Ahead: The Future of the Partisan Gap among Women in State Legislatures

Altogether, the results of the multivariate analyses underscore the central argument of the book and of this chapter, which is that the factors shaping the representation of women in elective office within the two parties are strikingly different. As a result, the future for the representation of women in state legislatures is both very promising and very disheartening. It is, quite simply, a tale of two parties.

For Democratic women, the future looks very bright. Women already form more than 40 percent of Democratic state legislators nationally, and every indication is that their representation will continue its upward climb. Democratic women's progress is being driven by a confluence of developments in American electoral and partisan politics, which have created an electoral environment favorable for liberal women office seekers. The ideological and regional realignment of the parties has resulted in a Democratic Party that is more cohesively liberal, where an increased number of women in elective office is viewed as a positive and important goal. This in turn has fostered a welcoming and supportive environment for the growing pool of working women with political ambitions. The political incorporation of women of color into state legislatures has also increased the representation of women in state legislatures, particularly in the South and West, and this development has driven gains almost exclusively among Democratic women. Finally, Democratic women are now benefiting from a reinforcing culture of recruitment. As the number of women in the party grows, the party's commitment to recruiting more women also expands. When openings emerge, Democratic women are well supported to take advantage of them.

Future prospects for the representation of Republican women in state legislatures are, in contrast, quite concerning. There is no one factor causing Republican women to wither in state legislatures but rather a confluence of long-term developments in American electoral politics that have created a challenging environment for Republican women office seekers. In many ways it is the Republican Party itself, specifically its conservatism and its reluctance to engage in group-based outreach toward women candidates, that is constraining opportunities for Republican women. As the party moved rightward ideologically and developed its power base in the South, progress for

Republican women legislators stalled, and today Republican women have their lowest levels of representation in Southern states and in states where the Republican Party is the strongest. The limited number of Republican women legislators constrains opportunities for women at higher levels of elective office and also the ability of the party to counter the image, hardened as a result of the 2016 presidential election, that the party is antiwoman. In contrast, as their party has become more southern and more conservative, and less supportive of the need for women in elective office, Republican women have faced an increasingly hostile and challenging environment.

Given that state legislatures remain the most common launching pad for congressional careers, the large size and continued growth of the partisan gap among women state legislators holds profound consequences for women's representation in Congress. The next chapter sets out to explore the role of the changing electoral landscape—the ideological, racial, and regional realignment of the parties—in the emergence and growth of the partisan gap among women in Congress.

3

Whither Republican Women?

Women in Congress

The 116th Congress convened in January 2019 to triumphant headlines celebrating the achievements of women. A record number of women ran for Congress in the 2018 midterm elections, and a record number won.[1] Women posted the largest ever jump in their numbers. Women emerged from the 2018 midterms forming a record 24 percent of Congress. Among the many historic accomplishments for women office seekers, the 2018 election resulted in women being elected to the US Senate for the first time in Tennessee, Mississippi, and Arizona and women being elected for the first time ever to House seats in Iowa and Pennsylvania.[2] The 116th House of Representatives also began its work with a woman, Nancy Pelosi, once again holding the top leadership position of Speaker.

The women of the 116th Congress are not just the most numerous in history but also the most diverse group ever to serve. There are a record forty-seven women of color serving in Congress, four in the Senate—Catherine Cortez-Masto, who is Latinx; Tammy Duckworth and Mazie Hirono, who are Asian Pacific Islander; and Kamala Harris, who is both Black and Asian and identifies as multiracial—and forty-three in the House of Representatives.[3] This includes a record-breaking number of Black women and Latinx women, including the first Latinas to represent the state of Texas. The 116th House of Representatives also includes the first Muslim women, the first Native American women, and the first women of color to represent four states: Connecticut, Kansas, Massachusetts, and Minnesota.[4] At just twenty-nine years old, Representative Alexandria Ocasio-Cortez, from New York, and Abby Finkenauer, of Iowa, became two of the youngest women ever elected to Congress.

Despite the triumphant headlines and the historic firsts, the goal of equal representation for women in Congress remains a distant one. A century after the ratification of the Nineteenth Amendment, which gave women the right to vote and a legal claim to equality in the political arena, women remain less than a quarter of the members of Congress. This means women's voices are dramatically underrepresented, as the US Senate holds confirmation hearings on Supreme Court nominees and as Congress considers legislation from health care to the Violence against Women Act renewal to funding for Planned Parenthood, policies that have disproportionate and disparate effects on women. Since presidential candidates, vice presidential running mates, and cabinet members often emerge from the pool of current or former members of Congress, women's significant underrepresentation in the House and Senate also constrains their opportunities for higher-level office.

Similar to research on women in state legislative office, many studies seeking to explain women's continued underrepresentation in Congress focus on women as a cohesive group, exploring factors such as women's relative presence, compared with men, in the congressional candidate eligibility pool;[5] women's relative lack of political ambition and confidence compared with similarly situated men;[6] and possible bias against women candidates among voters, party elites, campaign donors, and the news media.[7] Studies that seek to explain women's continued underrepresentation in Congress as a cohesive group, however, miss the dramatically different dynamics that characterize women's progress (or lack thereof) and levels of representation in Congress across the two parties.

The presence and progress of women in Congress, much like in state legislatures, has been a remarkably different story for Democratic women versus Republican women. The story for Democratic women is one of continued advancements in the House and Senate, and the achievement of meaningful representation within the Democratic Party caucus. The story for Republican women is one of struggle, backsliding, and serving only as tokens among their party's national legislators.

After reviewing the emergence and growth of the partisan gap among women members of Congress, this chapter draws on three of the theoretical frameworks presented in chapter 1—the ideological, regional, and racial realignment of the parties—to better understand the emergence of the partisan gap among women in Congress and the contrasting dynamics for Democratic and Republican women office seekers; the fourth framework, party culture and recruitment, is explored in the following chapter. These explorations into the causes of the partisan gap among women in Congress provide us with a fuller understanding of the key factors behind women's continued underrepresentation in Congress, as well as the factors that contribute toward gender equality in political office.

The Emergence and Growth of the Partisan Gap among Women in Congress

This chapter begins by looking at the trajectories of women's office holding in Congress, by party, over time. Figure 3.1 shows the overall number of women in Congress, combining the House and Senate over the past forty-five years. The good news is that women's overall numbers in Congress have grown from 19 in 1975 to 127 in the 116th Congress (2019–2021). The bad news is that the rate of increase has been very slow. Other than in 1992 and 2018 (each of which was labeled the "Year of the Woman"), when more women ran for Congress and won than usual, the number of women in Congress has only inched upward. If previous rates of progress continue, it could take until the end of the twenty-first century or longer for women to reach parity with men in Congress.

Figure 3.1 also breaks down the number of women in Congress, over time, by party. It shows that across the 1980s, there were roughly the same number of Democratic women as Republican women in Congress. Since the 1990s, however, women's progress in Congress has been powered exclusively by Democratic women. As of 2020, there are 21 Republican women in Congress, which is the same number of Republican women in Congress more than two decades prior, in 1995. Over the same time span, Democratic women's numbers in Congress increased by 70, from 36 to 106.

Figure 3.2 provides another lens into the emergence and growth of the partisan gap among women in Congress. It documents women's representation among congressional Democrats and congressional Republicans over time. In other words, this figure shows women's representation

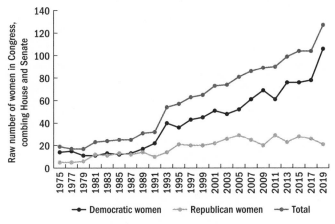

Figure 3.1. Women in Congress by Party over Time. *Source*: Center for American Women and Politics 2020e.

within their respective party caucuses, which allows us to make consistent comparisons, even as party dominance of Congress fluctuates.

In the late 1970s and across the 1980s, there were very few women in the US Senate and the US House of Representatives, but among the women who were there, they were represented in their respective parties at roughly the same rate. For example, in 1987 women formed about 4 percent of Democrats and 5 percent of Republicans. As figure 3.1 shows, women's progress in the two parties began to diverge across the 1990s. Democratic women not only made strong gains in 1992 but continued to post impressive gains throughout the remainder of the twentieth century and into the twenty-first century. As of 2020, women form 38 percent of congressional Democrats.

A very different trajectory characterizes Republican women over the same period. Women's representation among congressional Republicans stalled across the 1990s

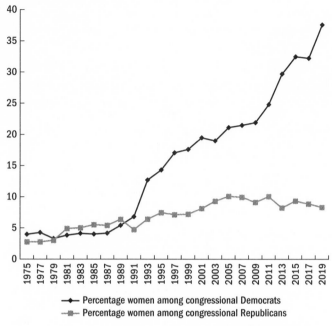

Figure 3.2. Women as a Percentage of Congressional Democrats and Republicans over Time. *Source*: Calculated by author using data from Center for American Women and Politics and Congressional Research Service Congress Profiles.

and into the twenty-first century. Republican women actually decreased as a portion of congressional Republicans in a number of election years, including the 2012 and 2016 elections. In contrast to the dramatic gains made by Democratic women, Republican women increased from 5 percent of congressional Republicans in 1987 to 8 percent of congressional Republicans today. Thus, the slowed progress of women in obtaining congressional office across the 1990s and the first two decades of the twenty-first century, rather than being some sort of roadblock all women office seekers have faced, was the product of challenges faced by Republican women only.

The 2018 midterm elections magnified the divergent trends of Democratic and Republican women in Congress. All the gains for women came from Democratic women, who increased their numbers by one in the Senate and twenty-seven in the House. In dramatic contrast, the 116th House of Representatives convened with only thirteen Republican women, ten fewer than in the 115th Congress. Today women form less than 7 percent of House Republicans and only 8 percent of Republicans in Congress overall. The one bright spot for Republican women in the 2018 elections was in the Senate, where they increased their representation from five to nine, which includes the postelection appointment of Martha McSally in 2019 and the appointment of Kelly Loeffler in 2020. Yet, even with these two recent appointments, the nine Republican women senators are far outnumbered by their seventeen Democratic women counterparts. As of 2020, 83 percent of the women in Congress are Democrats. While a partisan gap among women has characterized Congress since the 1990s, the 116th Congress has the largest partisan gap ever among its women members.

What explains the emergence and growth of the partisan gap among women in Congress? The partisan trends in women's representation in Congress shown in figures 3.1 and 3.2 are strikingly similar to those among women state legislatures, discussed in the previous chapter. In both cases, the partisan gap emerged and progress by Republican women stalled over the same period, coinciding with the parties' ideological realignment overall and over the issues of women's place in particular. As the Democratic Party affirmed and strengthened its commitment to gender equality in the private and public spheres, Democratic women continued to increase their numbers and representation among congressional Democrats. In contrast, as the Republican Party moved to the right ideologically and began to embrace more conservative positions on issues relating to women and gender equality, progress by Republican women halted.

Regional Realignment in Congress and Its Impact on the Partisan Gap

As discussed, one theoretical framework for understanding the emergence of the partisan gap concerns the regional realignment of the parties. Across the twentieth century and into the twenty-first century, the regional bases of the two parties have undergone significant shifts, with the biggest shifts occurring in the South. Klinkner and Schaller's analysis of regional realignment among House seats captures this well. In 1952, Democrats held 92 percent of House seats from the South. In the wake of the 2006 midterms, Democrats held only 40 percent of House seats from the South. The Democratic Party's dramatic losses among congressional House seats in the South, however, were coupled with gains in other regions of the country. From 1954 to the aftermath of the 2006 midterm election, Democrats went from holding only 45 percent of House seats in the Northeast to holding 74 percent while also posting gains in the West.[8] In contrast, Republicans made tremendous gains in the South, going from minority party to the overwhelming majority party, while losing seats in all other regions of the country.[9]

Given that geographic regions have long held implications for women's office holding in Congress, the regional realignment framework explores the impact that the regional partisan realignment in Congress has had on women's representation and the emergence of the partisan gap in particular. Table 3.1 shows women as a percentage of Republican and Democratic members of the House of Representatives and Congress overall, over a three-decade period, from 1987, a time when the partisan gap had not yet emerged among women in Congress (see figures 3.1 and 3.2), to the present, when the partisan gap is its largest size to date. This analysis is broken down into four geographic regions of the country: the Northeast, the South, the Midwest, and the West.[10] Because most analyses of regional realignment in Congress focus on the House, the data are presented both for the House and for Congress as a whole. Each cell in table 3.1 shows women as a percentage of their party caucus; beneath these percentages are the raw number of women Republicans/women Democrats, as well as the raw number of Republicans/Democrats from each region. The raw numbers allow us to see how much the regions have realigned between the two parties over this time period.

One of the most striking developments illustrated by table 3.1 has taken place in the Northeast. Prior to 1992, that region led the nation in its percentage of women in the US House of Representatives.[11] Table 3.1 shows that the Northeast was particularly welcoming to Republican women. As of 1987, Republican women represented 15 percent of their party's representatives and 12 percent of Republicans in Congress overall, a larger share than in any other region of the country and a larger share than their Democratic women counterparts. This statistic is even more impressive given that women formed only 5 percent of Congress at the time.

TABLE 3.1. Regional Realignment in Congress and Women's Representation, 1987–2019

	Women as Percentage of Democrats			Women as Percentage of Republicans		
	1987	2019	Net Change	1987	2019	Net Change
Northeast	House	House		House	House	
	5% (3/66)	30% (21/70)	+25	15% (6/41)	10% (2/21)	−5
	Congress	Congress		Congress	Congress	
	5% (4/80)	27% (25/91)	+22	12% (6/51)	17% (4/24)	+5
South	House	House		House	House	
	3% (3/89)	40% (20/50)	+37	0% (0/51)	3% (3/98)	+3
	Congress	Congress		Congress	Congress	
	3% (3/107)	38% (20/53)	+35	0% (0/59)	4% (5/121)	+4
Midwest	House	House		House	House	
	5% (3/62)	48% (19/40)	+43	6% (3/48)	7% (4/54)	+1
	Congress	Congress		Congress	Congress	
	4% (3/75)	50% (24/48)	+46	7% (4/60)	9% (6/70)	+2
West	House	House		House	House	
	7% (3/41)	39% (29/75)	+32	5% (2/34)	15% (4/27)	+10
	Congress	Congress		Congress	Congress	
	6% (3/51)	41% (37/90)	+35	4% (2/50)	16% (6/38)	+14
Total	House	House		House	House	
	5% (12/258)	38% (89/235)	+33	6% 11/174	7% 13/200	+1
	Congress	Congress		Congress	Congress	
	4% (12/220)	38% (106/282)	+34	6% (12/220)	8% (21/253)	+2

Note: Figures in parentheses are the raw number of Democratic/Republican women in the region over the total number of Democrats/Republicans in the region.

In line with the work of realignment scholars, table 3.1 shows that the Republican Party has lost political power in the Northeast. In 1987, there were fifty-one Republicans in Congress from the Northeast; over the next four decades, this number was cut in half, down to twenty-four Republicans in Congress from the Northeast. The trends in the House are similar. This loss of regional power holds significant implications for the partisan gap and the fate of Republican women. The Northeast has long been a region welcoming to women office seekers, especially Republican women. So as the Republican Party lost power and the ability to compete for seats in the Northeast, it lost ground in the region of the country most welcoming to Republican women office seekers, which has slowed progress for Republican women and, in the case of the House, actually reversed progress. Women have decreased from 15 percent of Northeastern Republicans in 1987 to only 10 percent of Northeastern Republicans in 2019. The reason women have been disproportionately harmed by the Northeastern realignment is most likely grounded in the types of districts Republican women tend to represent. Similar to the findings illustrated in the prior chapter, the typical district represented by a Republican woman is more liberal than the typical district represented by a Republican man.[12] This appears to have left Republican women more vulnerable to the negative effects of the northeastern realignment of their party.

While the Republican Party lost seats in the Northeast, it increased its congressional seat total by 62 seats, including 47 House seats, in the South over the last four decades, the biggest change in all regions of the country. Today the Republican Party dominates the South, holding 70 percent of congressional seats in the region (121 of 174). The results in table 3.1 are consistent with the hypothesis that the southern realignment of the Republican Party has had negative consequences for Republican women officeholders. The biggest opportunities for Republican gains in the House and Senate over the past three decades, as well as the most plentiful opportunities to run in safe Republican seats, have been in the region of the country most hostile to women's candidacies. In 1987 there were no Republican women in Congress from southern states; by 2019 this had increased to a mere three in the House and two in the Senate. Women form only 4 percent of congressional Republicans from southern states. Women's very low levels of representation among southern Republicans are all the more problematic given that the South represents the power base of the party. Thus, Republican women have their lowest levels of representation in the region of the country where their party is the strongest.

Meanwhile, the story behind the steady gains of Democratic women in Congress lies in part in the Northeast and in part in the West. As a result of the regional realignment, Democrats gained seats in the Northeast, with the Democratic Party now holding 77 percent of House seats from northeastern states. Although not as dramatic, the Democratic Party has also increased its seat total in western states. Women have been strategic and successful in taking advantage of Democratic opportunities as they have opened up in these regions. Democratic women formed only 6 percent of western Democrats in Congress in 1987; as of today they form 41 percent. Similarly, in the Northeast women increased their representation among their Democratic colleagues from 5 percent to 27 percent.

Interestingly, Democratic women also have made dramatic inroads among Democratic members of Congress even in the South and the Midwest, regions of the country where their party has lost seat shares. Even though the South has long been identified as the region of the country most hostile to women office seekers, it no longer plays that role for Democratic women. In fact, women have made tremendous inroads, increasing from 3 percent of congressional Democrats from the South in 1987, to forming 38 percent of congressional Democrats from the South as of 2019. Similarly, even though Democrats have lost seats in the Midwest over the past three decades, women have increased their representation as a share of Democrats. Thus, even in regions of the country that traditionally have been less open to women's candidacies, or where Democrats have struggled to maintain their hold on congressional seats, women have made gains. In other words, geography no longer constrains Democratic women in the way it does for Republican women. On the contrary, Democratic women are now making inroads into congressional seats in all regions of the country, just as they are in state legislatures.

The overall takeaways from the regional analysis framework are similar to those drawn in the previous chapter. While not the only factor, the regional realignment of the parties has played a modest role in contributing to the partisan gap among women in Congress. The realignment in the Northeast has taken a disproportionate toll on Republican women, while the growing power of the Republican Party in the South, the region least hospitable to women in politics, restrains Republican women from increasing their numbers. Meanwhile, as House seats have turned over and opened up across the Northeast, West, Midwest, and South, Democratic women have been strategic and successful at seizing these opportunities.

The Partisan Gap and Women of Color

A second, and related, framework employed to explore the emergence of the partisan gap is intersectionality—the ways that race, ethnicity, and gender intersect with partisanship and women's office holding. As discussed in earlier chapters, Americans of color were blocked from meaningful participation in American electoral politics, including office holding, for much of American history. The passage of the Voting Rights Act in 1965 opened the doors to increased political inclusion by Black Americans and other Americans of color. The act led to a dramatic influx of voters of color into the electorate and made it illegal for states to draw congressional district lines in a way to dilute the voting power of African Americans and other protected minority groups. In response to Supreme Court decisions interpreting the Voting Rights Act, state governments created more majority-minority congressional districts during each redistricting cycle, especially in the wake of the 1990 census. The creation of these districts has provided the best opportunity for individuals of color, whether men or women, to enter Congress.

These important legal and structural changes to American electoral politics led to a significant increase in representation by Black Americans and the Latinx community in Congress. In 1987, there were 38 people of color in Congress, House and Senate combined; as of the 116th Congress, there are a record-breaking 120 individuals of color in Congress, 9 in the Senate and 111 in the House.[13] The 116th Congress convened with 56 Black members (53 in the House and 3 in the Senate), 46 Latinx members (42 in the House and 4 in the Senate), 17 Asian American/Pacific Islander members (14 in the House and 3 in the

Senate), and 4 Native American members (all serve in the House).[14]

Reflecting their formal and informal exclusion from political institutions, as well as the double bind of sexism and racism, women of color entered national-level elective office later than white women and later than men of color.[15] The first white woman was elected to Congress in 1916, yet the first woman of color was not elected to Congress until 1964, when Patsy Mink was elected to represent Hawaii in the US House. The first Black woman was not elected to the House until 1968, when Shirley Chisholm won a House seat in New York, and the first Latinx woman was not elected to Congress until 1989.

Despite the institutional and structural forces that delayed their entrance into national-level legislative office, since the 1980s, women of color have increased their numbers in Congress at a relatively fast pace. In 1987, there were only two women of color in Congress, both serving in the House of Representatives. As of 2020, there are forty-seven women of color serving in Congress: four in the Senate and forty-three in the House of Representatives.[16]

In fact, since the 1980s, women of color have increased their presence in Congress at a much faster rate than non-Hispanic white women. Figure 3.3 shows women of color as a percentage of all members of Congress of color compared with the percentage of non-Hispanic white women among non-Hispanic white members of Congress, over time. This figure reveals that in 1987 white women and women of color were represented at about equal rates. Women of color were about 5 percent of all congressional members of color, and white women were about 5 percent of all white members of Congress. Since the late 1980s, however, women of color have achieved higher rates of

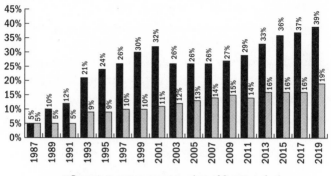

Figure 3.3. Women as a Percentage of Members of Congress of Color versus White Members of Congress

representation among lawmakers of color than white women have reached among white lawmakers. Today, women of color form 39 percent of members of Congress of color, while white women form only 19 percent of white members of Congress.

Table 3.2 breaks down the statistics illustrated in figure 3.3 by race and ethnicity. It shows that the comparatively stronger performance of women of color than white women holds true for all nonwhite racial and ethnic groups. In 1987, there was only one Black woman in Congress, and women composed 5 percent of Black members of Congress. Over time, Black women increased not only their absolute numbers in Congress but also their presence relative to Black men. In the 116th Congress there are a record twenty-three Black women, and women form 41 percent of the Black members of Congress.

The first Latinx woman did not enter Congress until 1989 with the election of Ileana Ros-Lehtinen. Today, however, there are a record fourteen Latinx women serving in

Congress, and women form 30 percent of the Latinx members of Congress. The statistics for Asian American/Pacific Islanders are quite stunning. Only one of the five Asian Americans/Pacific Islanders in Congress was a woman in 1987, but in the 116th Congress women actually form the majority of this group, nine of seventeen. The first Native American women were elected to Congress in 2018, and they represent two of the four Native Americans in the 116th Congress.

White women's progress has been slower than that of any of the other groups. Women form only 19 percent of the white members of the 116th Congress. Table 3.2 indicates that although women of all races and ethnicities (except Asian American/Pacific Islander) remain underrepresented in Congress in comparison to their male counterparts, the degree of underrepresentation is largest for white women.

The success of women of color in winning election to the House and Senate is particularly striking given the

TABLE 3.2. Women as a Percentage of Black, Latinx, Asian-Pacific, and White Members of Congress, 1987–2019

	1987	1997	2007	2019
Black/African American	5%	30%	28%	41%
	(1/22)	(12/40)	(11/40)	(23/56)
Latinx	0%	19%	23%	30%
	(0/11)	(4/21)	(7/30)	(14/46)
Asian American/Pacific Islander	20%	25%	25%	53%
	(1/5)	(1/4)	(2/8)	(9/17)
Non-Latino White	5%	10%	14%	19%
	(23/497)	(56/470)	(66/457)	(79/411)

Note: Top numbers in each cell indicate the percentage of women among each racial/ethnic category. Numbers below, in parentheses, are the raw numbers. All statistics are combined figures for the US House and Senate and are drawn from Congressional Research Service Congress Profiles.

double bind of racism and sexism they face.[17] Studies of congressional campaigns have, in fact, found that women of color receive less news coverage and less positive campaign coverage compared with white women, white men, and men of color, which places them at a disadvantage.[18]

The relatively stronger performance of women of color as congressional office seekers is driven by a variety of factors, but one of the most important appears to be that women of color have been particularly strategic and successful in running for newly created majority-minority districts as well as other open seats.[19] Table 3.2 shows that women of color made significant gains in the wake of the 1990 census, when the number of majority-minority congressional districts was significantly increased.[20] There is also evidence that Black women have higher levels of political ambition, that they are better positioned to tap into their own preexisting political and organizational networks, and that they may benefit more than white women from both racial and gender-based group solidarity.[21] Importantly, women of color also benefit from symbolic empowerment, high levels of support from historically marginalized groups who see themselves in their candidacies and feel particularly connected to their presence on the political stage.[22] Black women voters in particular have turned out in high numbers and given remarkably high levels of support for Black women congressional candidates.[23]

The strong performance of women of color relative to white women has contributed to the partisan gap in Congress because of the almost exclusive Democratic partisanship of the women of color in Congress. There have been seventy-eight women of color who have ever served in Congress, seventy-three in the House and five in the Senate. Of these women, only four have been Republicans: Patricia Saiki, Ileana Ros-Lehtinen, Mia Love, and Jaime Herrera Beutler. In other words, 95 percent of the women of color who have ever served in Congress have been Democrats.

While the 116th Congress broke records in terms of its racial and ethnic diversity, including the racial and ethnic diversity among its women members specifically, the Republican Party moved in the opposite direction, becoming a more white party. With the retirement of Representative Ileana Ros-Lehtinen (R-FL) and the loss of incumbent Representative Mia Love (R-UT), there are no women of color among Republican senators (there has actually never been a Republican women of color serving in the Senate) and only one woman of color among Republicans in the House of Representatives. In a dramatic contrast, the Democratic congressional caucus is more diverse than ever. There are a record four women of color serving in the Senate, and they are all Democrats. There are also a record forty-three women of color serving in the House, forty-two of whom are Democrats. In other words, 98 percent (forty-six of forty-seven) of the women of color serving in the 116th Congress are Democrats.

Taken together, the advancement of women of color and their higher levels of relative representation in Congress compared with white women combined with their almost exclusive Democratic partisanship, have played a modest but consistent role behind the partisan gap. If women of color were represented in Congress at the same, lower rate as white women—in other words, if women of color represented only 19 percent of those of color in Congress rather than 39 percent—there would be twenty-two fewer women in Congress, and likely twenty-two fewer Democratic women. Thus, without the strong performance by women of color in winning congressional seats, the partisan gap among women in Congress would still exist, but it would be considerably smaller.

Historically most of the gains in congressional representation for Black and Latinx women have emerged from majority-minority districts.[24] If the representation of women of color is tied to such districts, this could place a ceiling on the number of women of color in Congress and in turn their contribution to the partisan gap among women members of Congress. What is particularly striking about the women of color elected to the House of Representatives in 2018, however, is that they did not come primarily through majority-minority districts. As political scientist David Lublin has pointed out, eight of the nine black members of Congress newly elected in 2018 (as opposed to the forty-four black members who won reelection in 2018) won in districts that were majority white, and of these eight, four were women. The particularly strong performance of women of color relative to men of color in majority white districts can also be seen in the Senate, where specially drawn majority-minority districts play no role. Women now form four of the nine members of the Senate who are non-Hispanic white. This suggests that the strong performance of women of color is not limited to House districts drawn specifically to give political voice to racial and ethnic minorities, but extends to a broader range of political contexts.

Party Ideology and the Paths to Congress for Republican and Democratic Women

The emergence of a large partisan gap among women in Congress along with the partisan realignment over issues of women's place led to the hypothesis that Republican and Democratic women might be emerging from two different congressional pipelines. The ideological polarization framework, outlined in chapter 1, suggested that as the parties moved apart ideologically, and as the Republican Party grew more conservative overall and more traditional on the issues of women's place in particular, this may have had dampening effects on Republican women seeking office. In particular, working women and women with professional credentials may not feel welcome running in the Republican Party. In contrast, with its clear, prominent endorsement of gender equality in the public and private spheres, the Democratic Party may have emerged from this polarization better positioned to tap into the growing pool of highly educated women and professional women for US elected officials. To explore this idea, table 3.3 presents information on the educational, occupational, and political backgrounds of all the members of the 116th Congress, comparing women in the two parties with each other as well as with their men counterparts. After I examine partisan differences, I explore the paths to power through an intersectional lens in an attempt to explain how these paths are shaped simultaneously by the relationship of race/ethnicity and gender.

A college education has become a crucial informal requirement of obtaining a seat in Congress. Although less than half the US workforce has college degrees, almost all members of Congress have them, including 95 percent of House members and 100 percent of senators in the 116th Congress.[25] Although women were historically excluded from higher education, they have been surpassing men in terms of attending college and completing college degrees for several decades. Women now form half of the

TABLE 3.3. The Educational Background and Professional Paths to the 116th Congress, Broken Down by Gender and Party

	Democratic Women	Democratic Men	Republican Women	Republican Men
College degree	98	98	100	95
Advanced degree	74	81	48	64
Law degree	36	53	19	34
Legal career	34	49	22	30
State legislative experience	41	49	62	44
Political office-holding experience	63	71	81	63

Note: Numbers in cells are percentages and are based of analysis of all 535 members of the 116th Congress, including the House and Senate.

US workforce with college degrees.[26] Table 3.3 shows that there is essentially no difference across party and/or gender lines in terms of college degrees. Almost all of the women in Congress, regardless of party, have college degrees, and the same holds for men.

Holding a law degree has long been a common credential for those seeking elective office in the United States.[27] Even though women have caught up to men in terms of law school enrollments and graduation rates,[28] analyses of congressional membership in the first decade of the twenty-first century showed that men elected officials are still more likely than their women counterparts to list lawyer as their profession.[29] Table 3.3 shows that this gendered trend continues in the 116th Congress, with 42 percent of men and 33 percent of women members of Congress having a law degree.

In terms of paths to power for Republican versus Democratic women, what stands out is that Republican women are by far the group least likely to hold a law degree. Only 19 percent of Republican women hold a law degree, compared with 36 percent of Democratic women, 34 percent of Republican men, and 53 percent of Democratic men. There is a clear partisan divide in terms of paths to Congress, with Democrats overall more likely to have law degrees than Republicans (47 percent to 32 percent). Even taking that into account, however, Republican women members of Congress are by far the least likely to emerge from the growing pool of women lawyers.

Not surprisingly given the partisan/gender gap on law degrees, Republican women are also the least likely to emerge from legal careers, a category that includes attorneys and paralegals. Only 22 percent of Republican women in Congress emerged from legal careers, as opposed to 34 percent of Democratic women, 30 percent of Republican men, and 49 percent of Democratic men. According to an analysis done by the Congressional Research Service, lawyer is the third most common profession for members of the 116th Congress after public service/politics and business; however, table 3.3 shows that this pipeline profession is serving as an effective launching pad for Democratic women much more than for Republican women.

A similar pattern holds for advanced degrees more broadly. In the 116th Congress, 68 percent of House members and 77 percent of senators hold advanced degrees of some kind, and Republican women are comparatively underrepresented in this group. About 74 percent of Democratic women as opposed to 48 percent of Republican women in Congress have some type of advanced degree. Even after law degrees are taken into account, Democratic women are 9 percentage points more likely to hold advanced degrees over Republican women (38 to 29 percent). In fact, once law degrees are taken into account, Democratic women hold more advanced degrees than Republican men and Democratic men.

The fact that Republican women in Congress lag behind Democratic women in terms of possessing graduate
degrees and law degrees, and emerging out of legal careers, suggests that Republican and Democratic women
are coming to Congress through different routes. Moreover, it suggests that the eligibility pool theory (the idea
that as women come to form a larger portion of the people
with the high educational backgrounds and professional
backgrounds typical of elected officials their representation will increase) holds for Democratic women but not
Republican women. In other words, the significant gains
made by women over the past several decades in obtaining graduate degrees and law degrees appear to be disproportionately benefiting Democratic women with political
aspirations, and therefore contributing to the partisan gap
in Congress. In contrast, the Republican Party has not
been effective at recruiting or attracting women candidates from the growing pool of highly educated women
and lawyers.

Another important difference in the backgrounds of
Republican and Democratic women in Congress, which
lends insights into the partisan gap, concerns state legislative experience. Serving in state legislatures has long
been the most common path to power for members of
Congress.[30] This holds true for the 116th Congress as
well. Close to half (46 percent) of the members have state
legislative experience: 46 of the 100 senators and 198 of
the 435 members in the House.[31] It is important to note
that the state legislature is a well-trodden path to power
for both Democrats and Republicans, with 45 percent of
House Republicans and House Democrats having state
legislative experience, and 45 percent of Senate Republicans and 47 percent of Senate Democrats having state

legislative experience.[32] However, Republican women are the most likely of all the groups shown in table 3.3 to have state legislative experience. Republican women are more likely than Democratic women (62 percent to 41 percent) to come to Congress through the state legislative pipeline. Republican women's distinctively high level of state legislative experience holds true for each of the chambers of Congress. Moreover, Republican women's greater reliance on the state legislative pipeline is not unique to the 116th Congress but held true back in 2007 and even in 1987.[33] This is concerning because, as shown in chapter 2, Republican women have actually been losing ground in state legislatures. Therefore, one of the factors driving the partisan gap among women in Congress is Republican women's greater relative reliance on the state legislative pipeline combined with the reality that Republican women are a small, and in many states a shrinking, portion of the Republican state legislative pipeline. In contrast, women now form 40 percent of Democratic state legislators nationally. Their presence in the state legislative pipeline is robust and has been increasing steadily in all regions of the country.

Given the role women of color have played in the emergence of the partisan gap, as well as the profound role of both sexism and racism, as well as the intersection of the two, in shaping educational, career, and political opportunities in American society, it is important to break down the statistics in table 3.3 by race and ethnicity. Prior research has shown that congressional candidate emergence works differently for women of color than white women,[34] and that in prior years women of color have brought a different set of experiences and backgrounds to their congressional work.[35]

When we look at the paths to power among white, Black, and Latinx Democratic women serving in the 116th Congress, we see some important differences. Because there is only one woman of color who is a Republican, statistics are calculated only for Democratic women of color. Black women are the least likely to hold law degrees: 17 percent of Black women compared with 41 percent of white Democratic women and 42 percent of Latinx Democratic women hold such degrees. The gap in overall advanced degrees is much smaller, with 65 percent of Black women, 67 percent of Latinx women, and 77 percent of white women having advanced degrees. Democratic women of all races and ethnicities are more likely to come to Congress highly educated, with advanced degrees, than are Republican women. These statistics suggest that for the most part the eligibility pool theory is working to benefit Democratic women of all races and ethnicities and not just white women.

Black members of Congress overall are more likely to come to Congress with state legislative experience, and this holds true for women as well as men. Forty-four percent of Black women in the 116th Congress have state legislative experience compared with 39 percent of white Democratic women and 33 percent of Latinx Democratic women. Along similar lines, 74 percent of the Black women in Congress compared with 59 percent of white Democratic women and 67 percent of Latinx Democratic women have prior office-holding experience. The one Republican woman of color, Herrera Beutler, also has state legislative experience, but no graduate degree or law degree. Thus, women of color have taken different paths to power than white women, relying more on state legislative experience and prior elective office holding. While heavy reliance on the state legisla-tive pipeline may be problematic for Republican women, since their numbers have been decreasing, it may serve as an important asset to women of color. As discussed in chapter 2, women of color are overrepresented among state legislators of color compared with their white coun-terparts, and thus there is a robust and growing state leg-islative pipeline for women congressional candidates of color.

Conclusion

The 116th Congress convened to triumphant headlines touting women's historical accomplishments—the most women in Congress, the most diverse group of women in Congress, a woman Speaker—yet it also convened with the largest partisan gap among women elected officials in history. Democratic and Republican women started making inroads into Congress at about the same rate, but today Democratic women form an overwhelming 83 per-cent of the women in Congress. The progress of women in Congress over the past several decades has quite simply been a tale of two parties. Democratic women have made progress, but Republican women have lost ground. This chapter shows that no one factor by itself has caused the partisan gap, but that several overlapping and reinforc-ing dynamics in American politics have contributed to its emergence and growth.

Several factors have facilitated Democratic women's steady and impressive inroads into Congress. The regional realignment of the parties and the Democratic Party's expansion into the Northeast and the West, two regions historically friendly to women's candidacies, helped to create a supportive context for Democratic women office seekers. Additionally, the incorporation of women of color into the national-level politics, combined with the parties' realignment over racial issues, has led directly to comparatively larger gains by Democratic women over Republican women. The Democratic Party has also successfully tapped into the growing number of highly educated women, including women with law degrees, as congressional candidates. And, critically, the growth in the number of Democratic women as state legislators, the most common pipeline career for members of Congress, has boosted the representation of Democratic women. Today Democratic women form close to 40 percent of their caucus in Congress, which means women have a serious and significant voice at the table as their party crafts strategy and policies.

The story of Republican women in Congress is quite different. Progress among Republican women stalled at the national level during the early 1990s, about the same time the parties became clearly polarized ideologically and their divergent stances on women's place solidified. There are fewer Republican women in Congress today than there were a decade ago, and once again several factors contribute to this. The regional realignment of the parties has worked to the disadvantage of Republican women, as the Republican Party has gained power in the South, the region historically most hostile to women's candidacies. As an almost all-white party-in-government, the Republicans have not been able to benefit from the successes of women of color as congressional candidates. The Republican Party's growing conservatism has also resulted in its relative inability to tap into the growing pool of professional and highly educated women as candidates.

4

Left Out of the Party

Party Culture and the Recruitment of
Women Candidates

When women run for office, they tend to win at similar rates as equally qualified men, but women, more than men, rely on encouragement and recruitment from others in order to conceive of themselves as qualified candidates.[1] The fourth framework for investigating the partisan gap among women officeholders explores the way that the parties' distinctive cultures hold implications for the recruitment of and ultimately the representation of women in Congress. While some scholarship on political parties views the Republican Party and the Democratic Party as essentially mirror images of each other, the party culture theoretical framework views them as distinctively different entities in terms of the animating values of their members, their internal organizational structure and power flow, and their operational style.[2]

This chapter draws on a variety of qualitative data sources, including interviews with party organization elites, women candidates, and women officeholders, to explore the contours of the parties' distinctive cultures and examine the impact of party culture on the parties' level of commitment to, as well as their strategies for, recruiting women. While parties in the United States do not have control over their nominations, political parties, especially party leaders in Congress, and the parties' congressional campaign committees have taken on an increasingly active role in encouraging particular candidates to run and offering select candidates a range of valuable campaign support services.[3] Both parties also have extended networks of interest groups, political action committees, and activists that work in some degree of coordination with the national parties to recruit and support congressional candidates.[4]

At the national level, the Democratic and Republican parties have both indicated that recruiting more women to serve in Congress is one of their goals.[5] Parties have the potential to play an important role in terms of increasing the number of women office seekers because women are more likely than men to depend on explicit encouragement from others, especially party leaders, to spark their political ambition and confidence.[6] Barbara Burrell argues that while the parties, at one time, may have been a barrier to women's candidates, working to recruit men over women or seeking out women to run as sacrificial lambs in unwinnable races, this is no longer the case.[7] Both parties have launched informal and formal programs specifically designed to encourage more women to run. Moreover, both parties have extended networks of interest groups— including EMILY'S List on the left and VIEW PAC, Maggie's List, and Winning for Women on the right, that are specifically dedicated to increasing the representation of women in elected office,[8] groups that Crowder-Meyer and Cooperman label "women's representation policy demanders," or WRPDs.[9] Yet, the parties' distinctive cultures have the potential to differentially shape the execution and effectiveness of the efforts of the two parties and their extended networks of WRPDs to recruit women.

To assess the impact of party culture on national party recruitment efforts, and the recruitment of women to Congress in particular, this chapter draws on different sources of qualitative data, including interviews with national party and organizational elites, party strategy reports, and news coverage of related issues. During the months leading up to the 2014 midterm elections, I conducted twenty-one lengthy interviews with women members of Congress, women candidates, high-level congressional staffers and campaign workers, current and former members of the parties' congressional campaign and national committees, and high-level individuals working for organizations committed to recruiting and/or supporting women's candidacies. In addition to my own interviews, I was given access to the key findings from in-depth interviews conducted by Public Opinion Strategies for Political Parity, a nonpartisan organization committed to electing more women, conducted with ten Republican Party leaders and four Republican female members of Congress during March and April 2014. Those interviewed emerged from a combination of a purposive and snowball sample. I sought to speak to women members of Congress and their staffs, those involved with or knowledgeable about efforts to recruit women within the party organizations, and those working for nonparty organizations committed to electing more women to Congress, and then asked each of my interviewees to recommend others to interview. My interview data, therefore, provide a lens into the perspectives of those who are particularly committed to and/or affected by party efforts to support women.

The interviews with women candidates and members of Congress were particularly useful because these individuals were able to discuss firsthand the role their own parties played (or did not play) in their decision to run, their campaigns, as well as the activities their party leaders have asked them to take on in terms of recruiting, mentoring, and supporting other women candidates. Those working for nonparty organizations devoted to supporting women candidates were able to provide informed, and potentially more objective, outsider perspectives on the work the two parties are doing in regard to women's candidacies as well as providing insights into how these extended networks of WRPDs interact with the formal party organizational structures and members of Congress. Drawing on interview data collected during an earlier election cycle has benefits because it provides insights into the parties' strategies and goals in 2014 in terms of women's recruitment, and then allows us to assess whether these strategies have been sustained and the degree to which they have impacted the actual recruitment of women in subsequent election cycles.

In addition to original interview data, this chapter draws on a range of documents from the parties and from affiliated organizations committed to expanding the number of women in elective office. These documents provide insights into the methods the parties use to recruit candidates, as well as their rationale for wanting more women in office. I was particularly interested in comparing the public statements of the parties with the actual experiences of women candidates to assess the extent to which the efforts of the parties and their extended networks were substantive versus symbolic. Finally, this chapter draws on news media coverage of the parties' recruitment efforts as well as the experiences of women candidates. Particularly useful are media interviews with high-level individuals involved in recruiting candidates whom I was not able to interview myself, as well as more recent interviews with women candidates, women officeholders, and those involved in candidate recruitment. The combination of qualitative methods employed in this chapter helps elucidate the approaches of the parties toward the recruitment of women candidates and clarifies the role of the parties' distinctive cultures in shaping those approaches.

Democratic Party Culture and the Recruitment of Women to Congress

Jo Freeman's foundational work on political party culture in the United States characterized the Democratic Party as having an open and decentralized culture, where power flows upward, and where group identities and group-based activism are viewed as legitimate and valuable.[10] She argued that the decentralized nature of the Democratic Party culture made it particularly open to demands from previously marginalized groups, including women and racial and ethnic minority groups. In their more recent analysis of party culture, Grossman and Hopkins explicitly build on Freeman's analysis of party culture and argue that the Democratic Party is best understood "as a coalition of social groups seeking concrete government action" as opposed to the Republican Party, which is structured around ideology and more specifically conservatism.[11] In other words, the Democratic Party views activists making group-based demands and groups vying to shape party policy as the norm, rather than as an act of disloyalty toward the party or the party's liberal ideology. Cooperman and Crowder-Meyer further reaffirm this characterization of the Democratic Party culture, arguing that "the Democratic Party is essentially organized to hear and respond to group-based demands."[12]

The distinctively decentralized and open culture of the Democratic Party has a number of implications for the recruitment of women. Most important, it has allowed feminists and groups demanding increased representation for women to gain a strong foothold within the party's organizational structure. As Freeman describes it, it is not so much that feminists were welcomed by the Democratic Party, but rather that feminists marched in, made demands, and became a legitimate force in shaping party policies.[13] In this way, activists demanding women's representation became part of the fabric of the Democratic Party and were able to further pursue the goal of increased women's representation from within the party. Finally, the open structure of the Democratic Party has enabled it to partner productively with an extended network of groups, most prominently EMILY's List, that are single-mindedly focused on electing more Democratic women to office. This chapter now turns to discuss each of the ways Democratic Party culture has impacted the recruitment of women.

Increased Women's Representation as a Legitimate and Institutionalized Goal

The Democratic elites I interviewed agreed that group-based demands to elect more women were perceived as legitimate and widely accepted values among their party colleagues of all genders. As discussed in chapter 1, a majority of Democrats in the electorate agree that electing more women to Congress is a good thing and would benefit the nation.[14] This holds true for Democratic elites as well. In other words, the open and decentralized culture in the Democratic Party has culminated in a party at the elite and mass levels that is comfortable with demands for women's rights, gender equality, and the goal of explicitly recruiting and support women candidates.

This set of values, in turn, led to the creation of formal, institutional structures within the Democratic Party's congressional campaign organizations aimed at specifically supporting women candidates for both the House and the Senate. In 1999, the Democratic Congressional Campaign Committee (DCCC), which seeks to elect Democrats to the House, created a program called Women Lead. The program, which still exists, helps women candidates in competitive districts design and execute campaigns, as well as providing them with financial assistance. The Senate's campaign organization, the Democratic Senatorial Campaign Committee (DSCC) created a similar organization, which is now called the Women's Senate Network.[15] Women Lead and the Women's Senate Network are officially a part of the Democratic Party's national-level organization while also being led by women members of Congress and drawing on the expertise, advice, and time of other Democratic women in Congress to support women candidates. Those I interviewed explained how Democratic women in Congress are asked to mentor and answer the questions of women considering a run for Congress. In particular, they are encouraged to talk about work-family balance, especially if the candidate has young children.

While the Democrats I interviewed believed these programs could be and needed to be strengthened, many women candidates credit these formal party structures as providing them with meaningful campaign assistance and useful mentoring. For example, Senator Kirsten Gillibrand credited Representative Debbie Wasserman-Schultz, working as part of the Women Lead program, with helping allay her fears about running for office as a young mother when she was considering a run for the House.[16] Similarly, Katie McGinty, who ran a close but ultimately unsuccessful Senate race against incumbent Republican Pat Toomey in Pennsylvania in 2016, said that the Women's Senate Network helped her in every way, from "talking through the challenges in balancing a campaign and family life, and helping me to prepare my own girls for what the rigors of this are like, to opening their own Rolodexes and helping us build the resources for this campaign, to literally getting on the road with me."[17] Women Lead and the Women's Senate Network also offer women office seekers significant financial support. In 2018, for example, the Women's Senate Network raised more than $7.5 million, which was used to support the successful Senate bids of Democrats Jacky Rosen and Kyrsten Sinema, as well as the nine Democratic women senators running for reelection.[18]

Reinforcing a Culture That Prioritizes Recruiting Women

Interviews and other qualitative data suggest that Democratic efforts to recruit women are getting stronger over time, as more Democratic women enter Congress and get involved in the efforts. Previous studies and my own interviews underscore that most women members of Congress, regardless of party, are deeply committed to the idea of increasing the number of women in Congress. Women also tend to have more women in their social and professional networks, making the recruitment of women easier.[19] While this is true for women in both parties, what is different is that there are now many more Democratic women than Republican women in Congress who are in a position to engage in this recruitment and mentoring. Moreover, the number of Democratic women keeps increasing while the number of Republican women has gone down. For example, six Democratic women House members elected to Congress in 2012 labeled themselves "the pink ladies" and participated in Women Lead efforts during the 2016 election by taking every women recruit out to dinner and providing them with the support and advice they wished they had received from the party when they first ran for office.[20] Even if Republican women work twice as hard as their Democratic colleagues to recruit women, their efforts would still come up short compared with the Democratic colleagues, since there are more than five times as many Democratic women in Congress as Republican women.

In this way, the Democratic Party culture's commitment to gender equality is self-reinforcing. Freeman pointed out that party culture is in part driven by the experiences and the values of the party members.[21] As more women who are passionate about the goal of recruiting women become integrated into the party, the more deeply these values are embedded within the party's culture, which in turn shapes party behavior. Although the reinforcing dynamic of women recruiting more women cannot explain the origins of the partisan gap among women members of Congress, it appears to be a factor in the gap's persistence and growth. As one Republican woman member of Congress stated in response to a question about why there are more Democratic women in Congress, "I think it is a function of the numbers—they have more women. More women promotes more women. More seeds have more growth."

Democratic women with a strong commitment to and track record of recruiting women also have been elected to lead the party's congressional organizations, as leaders of the DCCC and the DSCC. The women who have held these positions have made recruiting more women a central priority. For example, Representative Nita Lowey, the first woman to lead the DCCC (2001–2003) was the founder of the Women Lead program in the House.[22] Representative Cheri Bustos, the current leader the DCCC (2019–present), also made recruiting, mentoring, and supporting women candidates, whom she views as having distinct needs and concerns as candidates, a priority in her work.[23]

Similarly, on the Senate side, Patty Murray led the DSCC two times and used that position to strongly prioritize the recruitment of women.[24] Several women senators, including Elizabeth Warren and Tammy Baldwin, credit Murray with reaching out to them very early on to encourage their candidacies.[25] The current leader of the DSCC, Catherine Cortez Masto of Nevada, came to the position after serving as the head of the Women's Senate Network. In contrast, the only woman to chair either of the Republican Congressional Campaign Committees was Elizabeth Dole, from 2005 to 2007, who was not particularly successful in the role and did not appear to emphasize the recruitment of women.[26]

Weaknesses in the Democratic Party's Efforts to Recruit Women

The Democratic Party's efforts to recruit women, while sustained, institutionalized, and supported by a growing group of Democratic women in office and party leaders, also have some weaknesses. Given the Democratic Party's significant advantage among women members of Congress, as well as its generally supportive culture toward the goal of gender equality and group-based recruitment efforts, I anticipated my interviews would reveal consensus that the Democratic Party organization at the national level strongly prioritizes the recruitment of women candidates. This was not the case. The majority of Democrats I spoke with indicated that while their party talks a good game when it comes to recruiting and supporting women candidates, it could and should do even more to take advantage of opportunities to recruit and support women candidates, especially women candidates of color.

First, because they are part of the Democratic Party's broader congressional campaign efforts, Women Lead and the Women's Senate Network are focused primarily on seats viewed as competitive in the general election, which leaves another opportunity for increasing women's representation—women running for open seats in safe Democratic districts—out of their purview. I spoke with one Democratic member of Congress, a woman of color, who indicated that when the safe Democratic seat in her district opened up, she never heard from the Democratic Party. Neither the DCCC nor those involved with Women Lead reached out to encourage her to run, nor did they offer her any campaign support. The DCCC, she pointed out, is not interested in spending its resources on safe seats. Rather, it was EMILY's List that called her, encouraged her to run, and offered her 24/7 campaign support and assistance. While the Democratic Party organization is willing to get involved in primary races in some cases (unlike the Republicans Congressional Committee, as discussed later), neither the DSCC nor the DCCC appears interested in using its primary endorsement power to prioritize an increase in the number of women in office over other goals.[27]

The Democratic Party's emphasis on recruiting and supporting candidates in competitive, swing districts disproportionately disadvantages women candidates of color, since they are more likely than white women candidates to be vying to represent heavily liberal districts that are not competitive in the general election. As a result, disproportionately more women candidates of color need to decide to run without party encouragement and need to navigate competitive primary contests without party support. Moreover, if women of color are successful in their primary bids, they often need to navigate their general election races without robust or consistent party support. Fraga and Hassell found that during general elections, white women receive more support from the Democratic Party than do men and women of color, a difference driven by the greater competitiveness of the districts white women tend to run in.[28] They conclude that Democratic party elites could be doing more to support candidates of color, including women candidates of color, during general election campaigns.

The Democratic Party's congressional campaign organizations are also, according to those I interviewed, more interested in winning races and supporting viable candidates than in supporting women candidates per se. This means that the formal party organization always supports incumbents over potential women primary challengers, and that the Democratic Party organization supports the candidates viewed as most electable and/or the best fit for the district, over the goal of increasing women's representation. Because electability is a subjective concept, this is an area where both gender bias and ethnoracial biases can seep into the work of the party organization. Several of my interviewees pointed out that the DCCC and EMILY's List sometimes endorse different candidates as evidence of the Democratic Party's lack of robust commitment to the goal of electing more women. While such scenarios are not common, there are multiple examples in recent election cycles.[29]

This weakness is also particularly problematic for women candidates of color. Several of the barrier-breaking women who won election to Congress in 2018, for example, were not recruited by the Democratic Party but instead gained their positions by running against established incumbents within their own party. Ilhan Omar (D-MN) won her first elected position in the Minnesota state legislature in 2016 by taking on and vanquishing a well-established incumbent in her own party and then running for an open congressional seat two years later.[30] Similarly, Alexandria Ocasio-Cortez (D-NY) and Ayanna Pressley (D-MA) gained their seats in the House of Representatives by challenging long-serving incumbents in their own party in primary elections.[31] Similar to the findings of Brown and Dowe from their interviews with Black women candidates, Omar, Ocasio-Cortez, and Pressley drew on their own political ambition, resources, and networks, rather than party support, in order to achieve their victories.[32]

The Democratic Party's advantage over the Republican Party in terms of the number of women in Congress also appears to have bred complacency among some Democratic party elites. The chair of the DCCC during the 2014 election cycle, Representative Steve Israel, stated the following in an interview with CNN in July 2013: "The difference between Republicans and Democrats is that they have to work hard to recruit women to run for Congress. All I have to do is answer my phone."[33] Such a statement from the person in charge of recruiting Democratic candidates is cause for concern given that women remain significantly underrepresented among Democratic congressional candidates compared with men, as well as research suggesting women rely on encouragement from others, especially party leaders, in order to conceive of themselves as credible candidates.

Finally, and importantly, one of the critiques Democratic party elites I interviewed offered was that the work of the DCCC's Women Lead program and the DSCC's Women's Leadership Network is overshadowed by the extended network of organizations committed to recruiting and supporting Democratic women candidates, most notably EMILY's List. EMILY's List came up in every interview I conducted, whether with Republicans or Democrats, underscoring how party elites on both sides of the aisle view it as the most powerful and successful organization committed to increasing political representation of women. Founded in the 1984, EMILY List's initial goals were to raise and bundle campaign funding for pro-choice women candidates.[34] Since then, it has evolved into "the preeminent campaign organization dedicated to electing female candidates," as well as a comprehensive, all-purpose campaign support organization for Democratic pro-choice women.[35] EMILY's List provides the women it endorses with crucial early funding and around-the-clock campaign support and guidance. While many other groups are seeking to increase the representation of Democratic women, they appear to view themselves as playing a supporting and complementary role to the work of EMILY's List.

Productive Partnership between the Democratic Party and EMILY's List

Even though Democratic elites viewed their party's efforts to recruit women as lacking in comparison with efforts by EMILY's List, the distinctive nature of the Democratic Party culture has played a role in allowing affiliated organizations such as EMILY's List to flourish and work in dynamic, integrated collaboration with the party. The party's comfort with group-based demands and its open and decentralized culture have created a party environment in which an extended network of groups committed to the election of Democratic women are able to develop a close relationship with the Democratic Party and become meaningfully integrated in its coalition.[36] Once again, this is not because the Democratic Party is naturally committed to the same priorities—interviews made it clear the party organization is first and foremost committed to winning elections—but that the structure allows women's groups to enter the party itself and demand attention. Moreover, because of the Democratic Party's essential comfort with groups competing against one other to shape policy, EMILY's List and other groups committed to electing women are able to single-mindedly pursue their agendas, even if it means challenging the Democratic Party's congressional campaign organizations, without being labeled disloyal and largely without fear of retribution[37]—which is not the case in the Republican Party. As a result of Democratic Party culture, EMILY's List has come to function much like an extension of the party. As political scientist Kelly

Dittmar points out, "In just over two decades, EMILY's List has gone from struggling to gain access to party leadership to becoming a party adjunct of sorts."[38] Echoing this sentiment, in an interview, a Republican official heavily involved in congressional recruitment stated that EMILY's List is now operating much like the parties' own congressional campaign organizations, describing it as a "mini NRCC."

The work of EMILY's List may even be behind the complacency expressed by some in the Democratic Party about how easy it is for the party to recruit women. After all, even if the Democratic Party does not recruit women, it has a strong extended network of groups that will do such work, and in many ways do it better than the party itself possibly could. EMILY's List fills in the problematic gaps in the Democratic Party's efforts to recruit women, discussed previously. Unlike the official Democratic congressional campaign organizations, EMILY's List plays an active role in promoting women candidates in primaries. Relatedly, EMILY's List is active in recruiting women in safe Democratic seats, which offer tremendous opportunities for women to make inroads into Congress and to acquire the seniority needed to advance to leadership roles, whereas formal party organizations focus their attention on competitive elections. Also, importantly, EMILY's List engages in consistent long-term recruitment, which is critical for developing women's candidacies, whereas the efforts of the Democratic congressional party organizations are focused on each discrete two-year election cycle. As Stephanie Schriock, who heads EMILY's List, stated in a 2014 *New York Times* interview, "Our job is to make at least seven asks" of every possible candidate,[39] a process that continues across election cycles.

Finally, the financial power of EMILY's List is vast and grows in each election cycle. Like the Democratic Party overall, EMILY's List and the growing network of groups devoted to electing Democratic women benefit greatly from strong commitment among Democrats, especially Democratic women, to the goal of electing women.[40] There are significantly more Democrats than Republicans interested in making donations to help get more women elected.[41] As a result, the extended network of groups committed to electing more women on the left significantly outraise their counterparts on the right. EMILY's List is often not just the top women's PAC but top the PAC overall in terms of supporting candidates in congressional elections.[42] The work of EMILY's List is not without its critics both within the Democratic Party,[43] and in the broader network of groups committed to electing progressive women,[44] but such disagreements are a cultural norm within the Democratic Party culture, rather than a sign of waning influence.

To summarize, the interviews and other qualitative data support the idea that the Democratic Party's distinctive culture has promoted the recruitment of women in several reinforcing ways. First, it has allowed feminists and those seeking to increase the representation of women in elective office to enter the party structure, to make group-based demands, and to have their demands viewed as legitimate. Second, as more individuals and groups committed to gender equality in public office became integrated into the Democratic Party, especially in leadership roles, they are able to reinforce and deepen the party's commitment to recruiting women. Finally, the Democratic Party's open culture, in which groups vie to shape policy as the normal course of action rather than as an act of disloyalty, has allowed it to partner productively with an extended network of groups, most notably EMILY's List, that are committed to increasing women's representation. Rather than seeing such groups as competitors or disloyal segments of the party, the Democratic Party has, to a significant degree, integrated them into the party structure.

Republican Party Culture and the Recruitment of Women to Congress

The Democratic Party is not alone in publicly committing to the goal of electing more women to office. For decades, leaders within the Republican Party also have articulated a desire to recruit more women to run for Congress.[45] For example, one of the first acts of Representative Tom Cole (R-OK), upon becoming chair of the National Republican Congressional Committee back in 2007 was to announce that he would like to recruit more women.[46] He asked then Representative Candice Miller to lead an effort to recruit women. In 2010, Representative Cathy McMorris Rodgers took on a similar role.[47]

The Republicans' loss in the 2012 presidential election and the sense that the so-called Republican war on women, including a series of unfortunate statements by male Republican candidates about gender-related issues, had contributed to this loss spurred a series of actions related to women's recruitment. A key action was that the National Republican Congressional Committee, the part of the Republican Party organization focused on electing Republicans to the House, created Project GROW, a program designed to draw on help from women members of Congress to recruit and support more Republican women congressional candidates. Although the NRCC had asked women members to undertake efforts to help recruit women in past election cycles, those I interviewed in 2014 emphasized that Project GROW was the first formal, institutionalized effort the NRCC had made to recruit women candidates.

My interviewees described Project GROW's strategy as consisting of the Republican Party taking several steps beyond the NRCC's traditional work around candidate recruitment. The first step consisted of asking, when a competitive House seat opened up, the question "Is there a qualified woman who could run for this seat?" and putting that question to county party chairs, chamber of commerce members, and other community leaders. One NRCC operative mentioned that while that might not sound like much, asking the question was something that the NRCC had not done previously. Next, if a qualified woman interested in running was identified, the NRCC/Project Grow would put her in touch with other Republican women in Congress who could answer questions she might have about running for and serving in Congress. Many of my interviewees felt that qualified Republican women were reluctant to run for Congress out of concern about the impact their campaigns might have on their husbands and children. Those I interviewed also felt that having women members of Congress talk with potential women candidates about the ways they balanced family life and public service was a useful way of overcoming this potential barrier and encouraging their fellow Republican women that they could manage a successful congressional campaign and career.

Yet the Republican Party's efforts at recruiting women, both formalized efforts like Project GROW and less structured but party-sanctioned efforts headed by individual Republican women in Congress, have been complicated and ultimately undermined by the dominant Republican Party culture. In contrast to the Democratic Party, the Republican Party culture is characterized by an emphasis on individualism, a rejection of group-based claims, and a vehement rejection of identity politics.[48] The party's culture is also characterized by a hierarchical structure, a top-down flow of power, and emphasis on party and ideological loyalty.[49] Unlike the Democratic Party, which is structured to house and respond to competing group-based demands, the Republican Party culture views group-based demands in a negative light, as both "disloyal and unnecessary."[50] These distinctive aspects of Republican Party culture hold several implications for the party's efforts to recruit women as office seekers.

Republican Party Culture Clash: Recruiting Women versus Gender Neutral Recruiting

One way in which the Republican Party's culture impacts the party's commitment to and strategy for recruiting women candidates is in the conflicting views expressed by party elites about whether the party should even be making extra efforts to encourage women per se to run for office. While some elites in the party say recruiting women is important, and some structures have been created to pursue such goals, many others believe strongly that the party must engage in gender-neutral recruiting,[51] which essentially means the party should not explicitly seek out women candidates. This results in tension within the Republican Party about how much, if anything, the party should be doing to recruit women.

On the one hand, a number of Republican elites truly think recruiting more women is important, if not critical, to the survival of their party. Among those who prioritize diversifying their party in terms of gender, there is agreement that thus far the party's efforts have been inadequate. Despite the party's emphasis on loyalty, a number of Republican party elites, notably women, have been willing to offer negative assessments of their party's efforts to recruit women. In a 2013 interview, when asked why there are so few Republican women in Congress, Liesl Hickey, at that time the executive director of the National Republican Congressional Committee, stated, "I think the party hasn't focused on it like they should have."[52] The same year, Sharon Day, cochair of the Republican National Committee, graded her party's efforts at recruiting women as a C.[53] Similar sentiments were offered in my interviews. Republican women House members made it clear that the national party organizations played no role in their emergence as candidates. The party did not encourage them to run or offer any type of support until they had won their primaries; even then, there was no effort to offer them additional support because they were women. As one Republican woman member of Congress stated, "There was no effort when I ran. It is a genuine effort. The only woman I was introduced [to] was Cathy McMorris Rodgers and Shelley Moore Capito when I ran, and that was through my own consultant. No effort was made by members to introduce me or help me."

In the wake of the 2018 election, when the number of Republican women in the House dropped significantly, from twenty-three down to thirteen, Republican women in Congress as well as in affiliated organizations committed to electing Republican women once again labeled the party's efforts as insufficient and underscored the need to do more.[54] Republican House member Elise Stefanik has been particularly vocal on this issue. She recounts standing up at a meeting with her fellow House Republicans shortly after the 2018 election and saying to them, "Take a look around. . . . This is not reflective of the American public. And you need to do something about it."[55] Importantly, in official documents and statements, such as the Republican National Committee's 2013 Growth and Opportunity Report, the national Republican Party has acknowledged that recruiting women not only is important but also requires greater and more explicit outreach efforts than recruiting men.[56] In other words, Republican Party leaders have recognized that if the party simply conducts business as usual and waits for candidates to throw their hats in the ring, the candidate pool will remain very male-dominated.

Yet at the same time, most Republican party elites are uncomfortable with such group-based outreach efforts because they go against the core values of the party's culture.[57] Emblematic of this sentiment is a statement by Katie Packer Gage, the deputy manager of Mitt Romney's 2012 presidential campaign and a partner at Burning Glass Consulting, a firm aimed at helping the Republican Party do better among women, who stated that Democrats have a "much more affirmative action philosophy" and that, in contrast, Republicans "want to elect qualified people, and if they happen to be women, that's a bonus. It shouldn't be the primary qualification."[58] In interviews conducted for this project, one Republican party elite stated, "I think to try to elect and recruit female candidates because they're female is a disservice to females. Having quality candidates is a priority." Even in the immediate aftermath of the 2018 election, when the number of Republican women in the US House of Representatives declined from twenty-three to thirteen, RNCC chair Tom Emmer warned against recruitment efforts that are "based on looking for a specific set of ingredients—gender, race, religion."[59] Thus, there is a lack of consensus within the party about whether making specific efforts to recruit women per se, as Project GROW and other less structured efforts have been designed to do, is even appropriate.

The lack of agreement in the Republican Party about the fundamental question of whether the party needs to or should explicitly recruit women works to undermine the party's efforts in this regard. Because party efforts to recruit women go against core tenets of the party culture, they end up being more symbolic than substantive,[60] significantly underfunded, and not sustained. A number of Republican women party elites whom I interviewed in the summer of 2014 questioned whether Project GROW was more of an attempt to combat the "Republican war against women" frame in the media rather than an earnest attempt to engage in the hard work of identifying, recruiting, and supporting women candidates. They pointed out that the sole individual at the NRCC tasked with launching and directing Project GROW when it was founded in 2013 was asked to do so on top of an already large portfolio, which consisted of outreach efforts to Hispanics and young people. By the summer of 2014, this person had already left the NRCC without any announcement of a new director.

Similarly, a Republican woman member of Congress who attended an event sponsored by Project GROW in 2014 found that it lacked substance. She stated, "I went to an event with Project GROW, and it was the most forced, artificial attempt to say we're working for women or trying to get women. It didn't feel genuine to me. It is almost like when someone is trying so hard, it looks fake." While Project GROW prioritized thirteen women candidates in 2014, five of whom went on to win election,[61] an NRCC official admitted in an interview that summer that Project GROW did not actually yield any additional women candidates for the 2014 cycle who were not already committed to running when the program was launched in 2013. In other words, the full extent of Project GROW's impact was to offer mentorship to thirteen women congressional candidates who had already decided to run.

As predicted by some Republican elites, Project GROW did not last long, operating as a distinct part of the Republican congressional campaign organization only through the 2014 election cycle before being subsumed under the Republican Party's Young Guns program, a subsidiary of the NRCC focused on providing extra party support and funding to well-qualified candidates in competitive races, but without a specific focus on recruiting women.[62] In an interview with *Roll Call* in 2015, Representative Richard Hudson, the NRCC recruitment chairman at the time, explained this change by stating, "The goal now is not to just go find female candidates and throw money at them, but to bring female candidates into the Young Guns program, so that we're helping them to develop as candidates so they can be more successful. . . . [Project GROW] was just running parallel to Young Guns, and now we want to run it with Young Guns."[63] The Young Guns program, however, does not have a specific focus on recruiting women candidates per se, and in some cases it has worked against them. For example, in the 2010 Republican primary for South Dakota's only House seat, the NRCC placed Blake Curd rather than Kristi Noem on the first tier of its Young Guns program.[64] After Noem won the Republican nomination, despite rather than because of party support, she too was named a Young Gun. Since 2016, when Project GROW was subsumed under the Young Guns Program, there do not appear to have been any efforts to specifically recruit women. Indeed, there were only three women in total in the Young Guns program for 2016 election cycle.[65]

The lack of unified commitment to the goal of recruiting women can also be seen on the Senate side, where there has never been a formal structure dedicated to recruiting Republican women. Despite the Republican National Committee's conclusion in the wake of the 2012 election that the party needed to take additional, proactive steps to recruit women, as articulated in the Growth and Opportunity Project Report, the Republican Senatorial Campaign Committee did not create any kind of formal organization focused on recruiting women.[66]

Therefore, in comparison to the Democratic Party, the Republican Party has had no formalized women's recruitment structure on the Senate side and only a short-lived structure on the House side. Driven by their divergent cultures, the Democratic Party therefore retains a structural advantage over the Republican Party in terms of recruiting women. The Democratic Party has institutionalized efforts to recruit women that have been in place for more than two decades, bolstered by a culture that views the recruitment of women candidates as a good and legitimate goal. In contrast, the Republican Party's ideological commitment to conservatism and rejection of identity politics has undercut efforts by the minority of individuals within the party who do see recruiting more women as a priority.

Despite the lack of infrastructure dedicated to recruiting and support Republican women Senate candidates, there is one relative bright spot in terms of the representation of Republican women. Women are actually better represented among Senate Republicans than they are among House Republicans. As of summer 2020, women form nine of fifty-three, or 17 percent of Republicans in the Senate. While this is still a dramatically lower level of representation than women have among Senate Democrats (women are seventeen of forty-seven Senate Democrats, or 36 percent), it is a much higher level of representation than in the House, where women form less than 7 percent of Republicans. Moreover, three of the nine Republican women currently serving in the Senate have entered very recently, in the aftermath of the 2018 election. This raises the question of why the Senate has been so much more hospitable for Republican women than the House in recent years. Is this trend an anomaly or something more systematic?

Rather than the product of any long-term structural changes in the electoral environment or party recruitment efforts, the growing number of Republican women in the Senate has been driven largely by the actions of individual Republican governors who have chosen to appoint women to fill Senate vacancies. In 2019, Governor Doug Ducey of Arizona appointed Martha McSally to fill the Senate seat vacated by Republican Jonathan Kyl, and in 2020 Governor Brian Kemp of Georgia appointed businesswoman Kelly Loeffler to fill the Senate vacancy in his state, driven in part by a desire to help his party improve its image among women voters.[67] These two women join Cindy Hyde-Smith, who was also appointed to the Senate in April 2018 by the governor of Mississippi and subsequently won a special election in November 2018, and Lisa Murkowski, who was appointed to the Senate by the governor of Alaska, who was also her father, in 2002.[68] Thus four out of the nine current Republican senators originally entered the Senate due to appointments rather than elections. While appointments are not an unusual way to enter the Senate, and those appointed to the Senate do accumulate at least some of the advantages of incumbents when they must run for their Senate seats in the next election,[69] the fact that 44 percent of Republican women senators have gained their seats through the appointment path is striking. For example, only two of the seventeen Democratic women in the US Senate entered originally through appointment, Kirsten Gillibrand and Tina Smith.[70] Appointment represents a significant route to the Senate for Republican women, but it is unclear whether such individual actions are enough to maintain, much less grow, the number of Republican women in the Senate. Two of the recently appointed Republican women senators—Kelly Loeffler and Martha McSally—face challenging elections with divided party support and uncertain outcomes in fall 2020.[71] Moreover, increasing the number of women through appointments is a viable strategy only in the Senate, and not the House.

Why Women Matter: Political Legitimacy versus Political Expediency

Given that a key tenet of Republican Party culture is the idea that group-based claims are illegitimate and unnecessary, many party leaders have been reluctant to argue that the Republican Party needs to recruit more women candidates because women bring a distinctive or valuable perspective, or because gender equality in public office is an important goal in and of itself. On the contrary, the rationale offered most frequently for party efforts to recruit women is that having more Republican women will help the party attract more votes from women and thus win more elections. When Representative Greg Walden, the former chair of the NRCC, announced the creation of Project GROW in 2013, for example, he stated, "Women are the majority, and we need to do a better job, and that's what this is all about."[72] Similarly, in an interview with *Time*, Andrea Bozek, a spokesperson for the NRCC, explained that a main objective of Project GROW is "to expand engagement to women voters through messaging, events and the recruitment of strong female Republican candidates."[73]

The Republican Party's emphasis on recruiting women candidates as a matter of political expediency, however, is problematic for two reasons. First, the idea that running women candidates will encourage more women to vote Republican or become Republican partisans is not supported in the literature.[74] Perhaps even more important, this message does not line up well with the reality of women's candidacies, which are more likely than those of men to be motivated by a desire to impact policy.[75] None of the Republican women candidates and members of Congress I interviewed mentioned anything related to political expediency when asked why electing more women is important. They all emphasized that having more women is important because women offer different and more practical perspectives on issues than men; that having more women in office helps create better policy; and that women officeholders are more focused than their male colleagues on solving problems and getting things done. In an interview, Republican representative Elise Stefanik also underscored the value of simply having more women at the table and argued that women Republicans are able to bring and have brought fresh perspectives to issues facing American families and women.[76] Thus, despite a party culture that disavows identity politics and group-based claims, many women in the Republican Party agree that women do bring something distinctive and important to the legislative process.[77] The disconnect between the party organization's interest in recruiting more women candidates to help the party win elections, and why women are actually motivated to run and what they feel they bring to the legislative process, which is to draw on their distinctive experiences and operational styles to shape policy and find solutions, also constrains the effectiveness of the Republican Party's efforts.

This tension has emerged, once again, leading up to the 2020 elections. Rebecca Schuller, head of Winning for Women, a PAC established in 2017 that is focused on electing more Republican women to Congress, stated in an op-ed that "party leadership at the highest levels is recognizing the importance of recruiting and supporting more female leaders. . . . These leaders understand that women aren't just important to the GOP politically and electorally. They understand that all Americans deserve a government that speaks to them."[78] However, Schuller's op-ed may reflect wishful thinking more than reality. In an interview with *The Hill* in May 2019, for example, NRCC chairman Tom Emmer continued to frame the Republican Party's need to recruit more women candidates in terms of pure political expediency when he stated, "The road back to the majority is through the suburbs, and the road through the suburbs is going to be with strong female candidates."[79]

Republican Women and the Challenge of Primaries

The Republican Party's cultural resistance to making explicit efforts to recruit and support women candidates holds particularly negative consequences for Republican women in competitive primary contests. Those I interviewed who were interested in increasing the representation of Republican women in Congress all identified primaries as a major obstacle. In their view, women are often the best candidates in terms of quality and electability in the general election, but they are not winning Republican primaries because male candidates have an easier time raising money. One Republican woman House member said this is especially the case in the South, where men with long records of making maximum donations to men candidates, when approached by a woman candidate, hesitate and say, "I'll have to ask my wife." Republican representative Elise Stefanik has also identified primaries as a key problem behind the withering numbers of Republican women in Congress. She indicates that as recruitment chair for the NRCC for the 2018 election cycle, she recruited one hundred women candidates, but most of them did not make it out of their primaries, and only one went on to win her election.[80]

Political scientist Shauna Shames has documented that perceptions about the challenges facing Republican women in congressional primaries are grounded in the reality that Republican women do in fact face higher hurdles.[81] Kitchens and Swers also find that in some cases, being a Republican woman competing in a primary appears to be a disadvantage in terms of fundraising.[82] Yet, the parts of the Republican Party organization dedicated to recruiting candidates overall, including Project GROW, maintain a party policy of staying out of primaries. Many of the Republican elites I interviewed felt that their party's lack of involvement in the primary stage, while a seemingly neutral policy, actually solidifies male advantage. In other words, the party's decision to stay out of primary races essentially gives the fundraising leaders, usually men, an advantage. As another Republican woman member of Congress stated, "When we have a quality leader who's running, there needs to be a commitment to get her through the primary. We've always adopted a hands-off approach to primaries."

Project GROW and other less formal efforts by the NRCC to recruit women have tried to circumvent the formal party prohibition against involvement in primaries by enlisting the support of Republican women members of Congress, who are free to endorse and fundraise on behalf of women candidates during the primaries, if they choose to do so. For example, the co-leaders of Project GROW, Representatives Diane Black and Ann Wagner, personally endorsed woman candidates in congressional primaries during the 2014 election cycle. In an even more ambitious attempt to work around the Republican Party rules banning primary involvement, Republican representative Elise Stefanik announced the creation of her own PAC, Elevate PAC, or E-PAC, in early 2019, which is designed to offer early financial support to Republican women in competitive primary contests.[83] In an interview with *Roll Call* shortly after the 2018 election, Representative Stefanik said, "I want to play in primaries, and I want to play big in primaries."[84]

The first comprehensive test of Elevate PAC's power to increase the number of Republican women in Congress will be the 2020 election, but past experience suggests the impact of this individual-based rather than party-based strategy may be limited as endorsements by individual women members of Congress may not hold the same value, symbolically and financially, as official party support and endorsements. In the 2014 election cycle, for example, the women candidates endorsed by the Project GROW cochairs did not win their primaries.[85] Moreover, Elise Stefanik's Elevate PAC had an early test in the summer of 2019 during a special House election in a safely Republican seat in North Carolina, and the results were not encouraging. Stefanik's PAC contributed the maximum amount allowable to the campaign of Joan Perry, the one woman candidate in the Republican primary. Stefanik was joined by all of the other twelve Republican women in the House in publicly endorsing and supporting Perry's candidacy. Yet, the political arm of the House Freedom Caucus backed one of Perry's male opponents, who went on to win the Republican primary and the general election.[86]

It is also clear that Representative Stefanik has had to fight against and challenge her party's culture to move forward with her efforts to support women candidates. Stefanik acknowledged in an interview with *Time* that she has been criticized by conservatives in her party who believe she is engaging in identity politics.[87] In response, she explains that she believes it is important for the Republican party-in-government to be more reflective of the American electorate. Also, although the NRCC chair Tom Emmer later went on to endorse the launch of Stefanik's PAC, his initial reaction was to criticize her plan to get involved in primaries as a mistake.[88] In a well-publicized exchange, Stefanik responded to Representative Emmer in a tweet that she was not asking for permission. This exchange, as well as the other criticism she has faced from fellow Republicans, underscores how Stefanik not only has had to work outside the actual Republican Party structure to support women candidates, but also has had to confront and challenge her party's culture in order to pursue her goal of increasing the number of Republican women.[89]

The Challenges Faced by Groups
Seeking to Elect Republican Women

There are numerous groups on the right that are committed to increasing the representation of Republican women in elective office. One of most prominent and long-standing of these organizations is Value in Electing Women (VIEW PAC), which was established in 1997.[90] There are also newer groups, including Maggie's List; which was founded in 2010, Republican Women for Progress, founded in 2016; and Winning for Women, which was created in 2017.[91]

As a result of the Republican Party's distinctive culture, however, the extended network of groups seeking to increase the number of Republican women in office has struggled to achieve acceptance, let alone influence, within the Republican Party. The party's hierarchical, top-down power structure and the high priority it places on party loyalty have created a power dynamic between these groups and the party that is different than on the Democratic side. Some of my interviewees working at organizations seeking to elect conservative women indicated that the Republican Party's hierarchical structure made them wary of taking on the party in the way EMILY's List has been willing to do on the Democratic side, and that their decision to act as good soldiers had, in the end, weakened their ability to influence the party. Republican leaders have been able to ignore their priorities and sideline their efforts. Additionally, the Republican commitment to individualism and its rejection of group-based demands place these women's groups in a precarious position. Several Republican elites I interviewed indicated that some Republican women are skittish about embracing their ties to groups committed to increasing representation among Republican women, given their party's skepticism, if not hostility, toward identity politics and groups promoting women's equality in particular. In this way the culture of the Republican Party has undermined the cohesion, strength, and integration of the extended network of groups devoted to increasing the representation of Republican women.

This culture has resulted in a lack of collaboration, some tension, and a duplication of efforts among the extended network of groups supporting Republican women candidates. One high-level Republican official stated, "We are almost hurting ourselves with all these different groups." Similarly, a Republican woman in Congress stated, "What I'm concerned about a bit is that you have NFRW [National Federation of Republican Women], VIEW PAC, Maggie's List—all these things—that I am concerned that there is not a truly coordinated effort and it will become too fragmented. I'm concerned that the RNC is not pulling it all together sufficiently to give donors and even candidates an idea of what the resources are. I wish there was more of a place to go to understand resources and help." As political scientist Malliga Och points out in her work on the feminization strategies of the Republican Party, "The efforts by the few Republican political action committees (PACs) who work on electing more conservative women to office are disjointed and have a small footprint."[92]

Perhaps most important, the extended network of groups focused on electing Republican women to Congress have struggled to raise funds, to expand their operations, and even to survive. None of these groups come anywhere close to EMILY's List in terms of fundraising and contributions to women candidates.[93] In the 2018 election, for example,

EMILY's List spent more than $100 million to support Democratic women candidates. In contrast, VIEW PAC, one of the longest-standing and most widely recognized of the Republican groups, has spent about $6.5 million over two decades of supporting women candidates.[94] Political scientists Crowder-Meyer and Cooperman demonstrate empirically that the Republican Party culture is a significant factor behind these fundraising challenges.[95] Conservative and Republican donors are much less likely than their Democratic counterparts to be motivated in their giving by a desire to increase the number of women in office. As a result, groups committed to increased representation of Republican women struggle to even remain in existence. For example, She-PAC was created in 2012 as both a traditional PAC and a super PAC, with the goal of contributing millions of dollars to Republican women running for state and federal office. Despite garnering considerable attention in the national news media, She-PAC raised very little money and lasted for only two election cycles.[96]

Additionally, the limited fundraising of the groups committed to electing Republican women constrains what these groups can do for candidates. Unlike EMILY's List, they are focused primarily or exclusively on providing financial contributions to women candidates. Campaign financing, especially early financing, is important and valuable for women candidates. However, by their own admission, the extended network of groups focused on electing Republican women to office simply do not provide anything like the full-service campaign recruitment and support that EMILY's List is able to provide. A repeated theme in the interviews I conducted with Republicans concerned about women's representation in their party was that the party needs its own EMILY's List, an aggressive and strong organization willing to get involved in the primary stage, not just in terms of money, but in terms of providing full-scale candidate support.

To summarize, several aspects of the Republican Party culture undermine its stated goal of electing more women to serve in Congress. First, explicit efforts to recruit women are supported by only a small faction within the party, which must fight against a dominant party culture that views such efforts as problematic forays into the identity politics of the left. Second, and relatedly, there is disagreement within the party about why having more women in office is important, which further undermines the party's ability to recruit and support women candidates. Finally, the hierarchical nature of Republican Party culture, with its emphasis on party and ideological loyalty, has undermined the party's ability to partner effectively with an extended network of groups focused on increasing women's representation in elective office.

Conclusion: Party Culture and the Recruitment of Women

While many factors contribute to the emergence and growth of the partisan gap among women in Congress, recruitment matters. The divergent cultures of the two parties have created contrasting environments for women seeking political office. The Democratic Party's culture has allowed groups seeking greater representation for women to enter the party and steer its resources and infrastructure in ways to help promote women's candidacies. In contrast, the Republican Party's strict adherence to conservative ideology and its top-down flow of power have complicated and undermined efforts of individual Republicans and the extended network of organizations committed to increasing the number of Republican women in office.

Increasing the number of Republican women in Congress will require a long-term, widespread, deep commitment among those responsible for recruiting candidates within the Republican Party. Although some individuals within the Republican Party and its extended network are highly committed to this goal, there does not appear to be cohesive support for the goal, nor does it appear to be a priority for party leadership. Since the disappearance of Project GROW, the Republican Party has not developed a formal plan or infrastructure for recruiting more women candidates. Several Republican governors have taken individual steps to increase the number of Republican women in elective office by appointing women to fill vacated Senate seats. Similarly, Republican women in the House remain interested in taking action to increase their numbers, as shown by their unified support of Joan Perry in the special election congressional primary that took place in summer 2019 and by their support of Representative Elise Stefanik's Elevate PAC. But their actions alone are unlikely to overcome the broader obstacles presented by their party's culture, which is characterized by a commitment to gender-neutral recruiting, a belief that recruiting women is useful only for reasons of political expediency, and a wariness of external groups designed to increase women's representation.

Additionally, Republican women in Congress face a tough electoral landscape going forward. Heading into the 2020 election, there are only thirteen Republican women in the House, and two of them, Susan Brooks and Martha Roby, have already announced plans to retire. On the Senate side, there are now nine Republican women in the

Senate, four of whom face tough reelection fights—Susan Collins of Maine, Martha McSally of Arizona, Kelly Loeffler of Georgia, and Joni Ernst of Iowa. Thus, the Republican Party will need to recruit and elect more women than it did in 2018 even to hold steady its already comparatively small numbers, let alone increase the representation of Republican women in Congress.

In contrast, women form a critical mass within the Democratic Party in both the House and the Senate, and women appear to be on track to continue increasing their representation within the Democratic party-in-government. As more women take on leadership positions within the Democratic Party, the chances of recruiting more women candidates grows. Institutionalized efforts to recruit Democratic women, including Women Lead in the House and the Women's Senate Network—both started and headed by Democratic women in Congress[97]—are energized by their recent successes, and their efforts are supported by the highest levels of party leadership. The 2020 election and beyond, therefore, seem likely to bring our nation a few steps closer to an even more pronounced gendering of the parties-in-government, which will significantly shape both the substance and the appearance of American politics.

Conclusion

The Future of the Partisan Gap among Women in Office

This book began with a puzzle regarding women's representation in elective office. Democratic women are on a steady march toward equal representation in state legislatures, the US House of Representatives, and the US Senate. There are now more Democratic women in elective office than at any previous point in the nation's history. The Democratic women in elected office are highly diverse in terms of their age, race, and ethnicity; they are a highly visible symbol of the diversity of the United States. Yet, while Democratic women have been making steady, impressive progress, gains for Republican women in elective office have stalled and in many cases reversed. Republicans head into the 2020 elections with a congressional membership that is 92 percent male and 95 percent white.

Why do patterns of legislative office holding among women vary so dramatically across the two parties? What factors drive the steady progress of Democratic women? And why is the representation of Republican women withering, even as women are making tremendous strides in terms of educational and professional attainment? The central argument of this book is that several long-term, structural changes in American electoral politics— the ideological polarization of the parties, the regional realignment of the parties' geographic bases, and the political incorporation of Americans of color into elective office, combined with partisan realignment over issues of race and civil rights—have had a profound impact on the representation of women in political office. These reinforcing trends have reshaped the electoral landscape and the parties' respective cultures and in doing so have led to the emergence and growth of the partisan gap among women state legislators and women in Congress. As the parties have realigned regionally, ideologically, and in terms of race, the electoral environment facing Democratic women has become much more welcoming and supportive. In contrast, these structural changes in the American political landscape have resulted in Republican women office seekers facing an increasingly hostile and less supportive environment.

The Presidency of Donald Trump and the Widening Partisan Gap among Women in Elective Office

An important issue that needs to be addressed is how the 2016 presidential election and the presidency of Donald Trump factor into this argument and the future of the partisan gap among women in elective office. The defeat of Hillary Clinton, the first woman major party candidate for president, combined with the election of Donald Trump, who has a history of sexist and misogynistic actions and statements, led to a significant political mobilization among progressive women. President Trump's inauguration was followed by one of the largest women's marches in history.[1] It also led a number of Democratic women to consider running for political office who had not previously considered the idea, without having any parallel effect on political ambition among Republican women.[2] The victory of Donald Trump in the 2016 presidential election was an explicit factor in the decision-making calculus of many of the record number of Democratic women who ran for state legislative and congressional seats in the 2018 election.[3]

In contrast, Trump's election appears to have inflicted further damage to the already low levels of representation of women among Republicans in elective office. His unpopularity overall and in suburban areas in particular had a disproportionately negative impact on Republican women officeholders and candidates in the 2018 midterm elections and contributed to the dramatic drop of Republican women in the House of Representatives and the decline in the number of Republican women in state legislatures.[4] In other words, even though a majority of white women and an overwhelming majority of white Republican women supported Donald Trump in the 2016 election—as they have supported other recent Republican presidential candidates[5]—Trump's election appears to have worked against the representation of conservative women in elective office.

In these ways—by disproportionately motivating Democratic women to run for office and by contributing to Republican losses in ideologically moderate, suburban areas, where Republican women disproportionately hold office—Trump's presidency has exacerbated the partisan gap among women in office. But neither the 2016 presidential election nor the presidency of Donald Trump created the partisan gap. As this book details, the partisan gap among women in elective office is not a recent phenomenon. The numerical advantage of Democratic women over Republican women in Congress and state legislatures emerged in the early 1990s and has been growing larger for three decades and counting. Changes in the electoral landscape that have been underway for decades, much longer than Donald Trump has been on the national political scene, are behind these contrasting party dynamics.

The structural forces behind the partisan gap also mean that the partisan gap among women in elective office will continue after the presidency of Donald Trump and well into the twenty-first century. Indeed, the theoretical frameworks employed in this book not only help to account for the emergence and growth of the partisan gap but also offer a very clear prediction: the partisan gap among women in elective office, already historic in size, will continue to grow in size. The ideological, regional, and racial realignments that have driven the partisan gap among women in state legislatures, the House of Representatives, and the Senate show no signs of reversing. On the contrary, these dynamics continue to unfurl in ways that predict a further widening of the already historic gap between the representation of Democratic women and Republican women in elective office.

Women are already represented at rates proportionate to their presence in the US population in the Democratic caucus in many state legislatures, and women appear on track to achieve, if not surpass, parity among Democratic officeholders. Yet on the other side of the partisan aisle, prospects for Republican women look dim. Republican women's representation has withered rather than grown, and it is possible that the 2020 election and beyond could further extend this downward trend.

The ideological polarization of the parties, characterized by the Republican Party's significant shift to the right combined with the Democratic Party's movement to the left, is a well-known, highly analyzed, and much lamented development in American society. Scholars have documented its many impacts on American politics. Partisan polarization has contributed to legislative gridlock, deepened distrust of government, and fostered a more acrimonious political discourse. What this book demonstrates is that ideological polarization of the parties also has had significant implications for the emergence and growth of the partisan gap among women in state legislatures and Congress. Conservatism, once correlated with lower levels of women's representation overall, acting as an obstacle for both Democratic and Republican women, now constrains the representation of Republican women legislators only.

The Republican Party's embrace of more traditional views on the role of women has made it a less welcoming home for the growing number of working women, women who have the resources and networks, as well as the educational and professional credentials, that are informal prerequisites for legislative careers. A record number of women have been obtaining college degrees, law degrees, and other advanced degrees. By championing policies that help working women and highlighting the importance of gender equality in the private and public spheres, the Democratic Party has been able to effectively tap into this growing pool of potential women candidates, which in turn drives the representation of women in the Democratic Party upward. In contrast, the Republican Party's conflicting views on the appropriate role of women, as well as the need for gender equality in political office, have made the party a less welcoming home for working and professional women with political ambitions. The ideological polarization of the parties will continue to shape the electoral terrain faced by women office seekers in the post-Trump era, making it highly likely that the partisan gap among women in elective office will continue to expand.

Racial and Regional Realignments and the Future of Women in Elective Office

The incorporation of Americans of color into elective political office and the racial realignment of the parties have been immensely consequential in American politics. The almost complete exclusion of women of color from political office holding is just one example of how the intersection of institutionalized racism and sexism has structured American democracy since the nation's founding. Conversely, the growing diversity of elected officials is a dramatic illustration of how our nation has become more democratic over time. This book also shows that the eventual incorporation of women of color into elective office has contributed to the emergence of the partisan gap, by driving increased representation of Democratic women in state legislatures and Congress. Although women candidates and legislators of color have faced formidable barriers, both historically and in current times, they have increased their representation in elective office at a faster rate than white women. In particular, the strong performance of Black women in obtaining seats in state legislatures and the US House of Representatives helps explain the impressive gains by Democratic women in state legislatures and congressional delegations in southern states, a region of the country historically unwelcoming to women's candidacies due to its traditional views and conservative culture.

The ideological, racial, and regional realignments of the parties are intimately intertwined, and their interplay has resulted in Republican women office seekers facing a particularly challenging environment in areas where their party offers the most plentiful opportunities for office holding. The South, the region of the country most unwelcome to women's candidates, continues to be the region holding the most promise for future Republican gains, and this constrains opportunities for Republican women office seekers. There are some signs that the contours of the southern realignment may be evolving, and that Democrats are gaining ground and may soon be competitive on a statewide level in states such as Georgia, North Carolina, and even Texas. The competitiveness of the Democratic Party in southern states is driven in part by the great reverse migration of Black Americans to southern states and the growing number of Black voters who turn out in strong numbers to support Democratic candidates, especially Black Democratic candidates.[6] The evolving partisan realignment in the South is likely to result in the election of even more Black Democratic women to state legislatures and Congress while either having no impact or further reducing the already slim opportunities for Republican women candidates in southern states, which in turn will further magnify the already strikingly large partisan gap among women in elective office.

If the Republican Party was able to attract a greater share of the Asian American, Latinx, and African American women interested in pursuing political careers to run as Republicans, the partisan gap among women in elective office would shrink. Such a development seems unlikely, however, given the nature of partisan competition in the United States.[7] The partisan realignment over race, which unfolded across the twentieth century, is not a historical development but continues to unfold through the present, with the Republican Party adopting policies and rhetoric that further alienate people of color rather than inviting them into the party. The Republican Party has increasingly become a home to those for whom white identity is important, as well as those motivated by racial and ethnic resentment.[8]

One of many important implications of this continued realignment has been that Americans of color in elective office are increasingly identifying as Democrats, while the Republican party-in-government has become even more overwhelmingly white. The 2018 elections resulted not only in the loss of Republican women but also in the loss of Republican women of color in both state legislatures and the House of Representatives. Representative Will Hurd, the only Black Republican in the 116th House of Representatives, has announced he will not seek another term, thereby furthering this trend. It seems safe to predict that for decades into the future, the Democratic Party will remain the exclusive beneficiary of the strong performance of women of color as congressional and state legislative candidates, while the Republican Party will remain the home of a small and potentially shrinking group of conservative white women officeholders.

Some have speculated that the strong relationship between the representation of Black and Latinx Americans and the existence of majority-minority legislative districts could put a ceiling on further electoral gains by Americans of color overall and women in particular. The redistricting of legislative seats that will take place in the wake of the 2020 census may even result in a reduction in the number of majority-minority districts. Since one of the drivers of the partisan gap among women in elective office has been the faster rate of growth among women legislators of color compared with white women, this aspect of the electoral landscape of the 2020s could potentially slow the growth of the partisan gap.

Yet there are also compelling reasons to think the future of women of color in politics may not be tied to majority-minority districts, as it has been historically, and thus their strong performance will continue to drive the partisan gap even wider. Recent research shows that Black candidates can now win in districts that do not have a majority of Black voters.[9] More than one-third of women of color who were elected to the US House for the first time in 2018 won in districts that had a majority of white voters.[10] Additionally, the American electorate is becoming more racially and ethnically diverse, while whites are declining as a share of the electorate. This means that the portion of Latinx, Asian American, and Black voters in legislative districts will increase even without the explicit drawing of majority-minority districts. While there are potential downsides to the close relationship of communities of color and the Democratic Party, such as reduced leverage to influence policy and strategy,[11] this strong relationship predicts that the partisan gap among women in office will likely grow bigger as the Democratic Party exclusively benefits from the strategic and successful candidacies of women of color.

The Blue Wave and the Widening Partisan Gap among Women in Elective Office

The "blue wave," or strong levels of Democratic partisanship among young Americans, also seems likely to further the partisan gap among women officeholders in the coming decades. During the Obama years, young people emerged as a disproportionately Democratic group in terms of their vote choice. Some questioned whether the relationship between young Americans and the Democratic Party was uniquely tied to the presidency of Barack Obama or whether it was part of a longer-term alignment among young people with the Democratic Party. Voting patterns from the 2018 midterm elections suggest that the overwhelmingly Democratic partisanship of young people is continuing beyond the Obama presidency. According to data from the Center for Information and Research on Civic Learning and Engagement (CIRCLE), 67 percent of young voters supported Democratic House candidates in 2018, which is an even higher percentage than supported Democrats in 2008 when Barack Obama was on the ballot for the first time. CIRCLE has also tracked a meaningful increase in political protest and marches by young people, especially young people who are registered Democrats.[12] While voting and protesting are distinct forms of participation from running for office, these statistics suggest that young people overall, and young women in particular, who eventually decide to run for elective office will be a disproportionately Democratic group. Once again this portends a further widening of the partisan gap among women in elective office.

Will 2020 Be the Year of the Republican Woman?

Despite the many structural trends pointing toward a further widening of the gap between the representation of Democratic and Republican women in office, a spate of stories in the news media have suggested that 2020 is on track to be an unprecedentedly good year for Republican women as office seekers, and that 2020 may result in a narrowing of the partisan gap. NBC News ran a story about the 2020 election titled "More Republican Women Than Ever Are Planning to Run for Office." A spokesperson for the National Republican Campaign Committee said that the committee met with an unprecedented number of Republican women who expressed interest in running for Congress in 2020.[13] The executive director of the Women's Campaign School at Yale University also said that she has been fielding more calls from Republican women than ever before. Julie Conway, the head of VIEW PAC, one of the longest-running organizations working to increase the number of Republican women in Congress, has also said she has met with more Republican women than usual who are seriously considering congressional bids.[14] These predictions have in fact been borne out by a record number of Republican women filing to run for congressional seats in the 2020 election.[15]

Those interviewed provided a number of reasons to explain the uptick in political ambition among Republican women. Some of the women who are running say that they are doing so to protect Republican women from extinction. Others say they are motivated by a desire to explicitly counter Donald Trump's derogatory comments about and toward women. Additionally, some women state that they are inspired by the dramatic successes of Democratic women in the 2018 election.[16] These stories, combined with profiles of Elise Stefanik and her PAC designed to help Republican women win their primary races, have been pulled together to argue that much as 2018 was the year of the Democratic woman, 2020 may be the year of the Republican woman.

News stories about potential breakthroughs by Republican women in elective office stand in contrast with the central argument advanced in this book, which posits that 2020 is unlikely to be the year of Republican women. Even though more Republican women than ever have filed to run for Congress in 2020, they have to navigate a challenging landscape, including a party culture and an electoral environment that are hostile to their candidacies. While the efforts of groups dedicated to increasing the representation of Republican women, including VIEW PAC and Winning for Women, as well as the work of Republican Elise Stefanik, are genuine, valuable steps toward increasing the number of Republican women in office, these actions alone are unlikely to shift the trajectory of the partisan gap. Structural forces underlie this gap—the conservatism of the party, its regional stronghold in the South, and its whiteness—and there are no signs these trends are changing. Further, the distinctive cultures of the parties, documented in the 1980s by political scientist Jo Freeman and further confirmed and illustrated in more recent research,[17] have also resulted in a distinctively more favorable environment for Democratic women office seekers than for their Republican counterparts.

To shift the trajectory of Republican women in office, and meaningfully increase women's representation among Republicans in state legislatures and Congress, it will take a serious effort by the Republican Party to create a robust, sustained, and institutionalized infrastructure dedicated to consciously, aggressively, and proactively recruiting women and supporting women office seekers at the state and national levels and more effectively partnering with existing organizations interested in these same goals. Perhaps not surprisingly given the culture of the Republican Party, which is committed to individualism and letting the best candidates find the party rather than targeting specific groups, there are no signs that this is happening. Despite NRCC chair Tom Emmer saying there will be a "woman's program" for the 2020 election, no formal structure within the Republican Party organization has been established.[18] Indeed, when asked about the party's low numbers of women in Congress, at an event celebrating the launch of Representative Stefanik's Elevate PAC, Republican House minority whip Steve Scalise argued that the Democratic Party was to blame, rather than identifying any ways the Republican Party's culture or recruitment strategy needed to change. Representative Scalise stated, "I've noticed that when female members run on the Republican side, Nancy Pelosi will spend a lot more money, in many cases twice as much more to defeat Republican female candidates in [sic] incumbents." He went on to add that "Nancy Pelosi does not want our party to look diverse."[19] The Democratic Party's congressional campaign organizations do heavily target swing districts, and Republican women are disproportionately represented in such districts, but blaming the Democratic Party for the lack of diversity in the Republican Party misses the structural factors that have driven the partisan gap.

In interviews, Democratic women actually say they would very much like to see more Republican women in office.[20] In part this is because women in Congress feel that they can work effectively with other women, and also because women in office realize that unless representation by Republican women increases, women will never be able to reach parity in elected office. The distance between the actual structural causes for the struggles of Republican women in achieving representation and the understanding of this issue by Republican leaders suggests that the Republican Party is not well positioned to begin closing the gap.

The Image of the Parties and the Self-Reinforcing Aspects of the Partisan Gap

The partisan gap is also on track to grow further because it has become a self-reinforcing phenomenon. This gap has a clear upward-reinforcing effect in that the partisan gap among women in lower levels of elective office shapes the candidate pool and hence the partisan gap among women at higher levels of office. Serving in state legislatures has for decades been the most common pipeline profession of members of Congress. While women and men used to take different routes to Congress, women's paths have come increasingly to resemble those of men, including a heavy reliance on state legislative experience.[21] In fact, state legislative experience is now more common among women than men in Congress, with Republican women the most likely of all groups to have emerged from the state legislative pipeline. While state legislative experience can be a valuable asset, this pattern has clear implications for the partisan gap among women in Congress. Democratic women are a robust and growing presence in the state legislative pipeline, which in turn helps drive their numbers upward in Congress. In contrast, Republican women are not well represented in the state legislative pipeline. The number of Republican women in state legislatures is actually lower than it was twenty-five years ago.[22] Moreover, Republican women have their lowest levels of representation in heavily Republican states, where opportunities for advancement to higher office for Republicans are most robust. Thus, the struggle of Republican women in state legislatures is constraining them at the national level.

We also see the upward-reinforcing effects of the partisan gap in the 2020 presidential race. Being a member of

Congress has long been one of the main launching pads for presidential campaigns. Indeed, all of the Democratic presidential candidates over the past five election cycles, from 2000 to the present, have had congressional experience, including the first woman major party presidential candidate, Hillary Clinton. Therefore, the fact that Democrats form 83 percent of the women in Congress holds implications for women's presence as presidential candidates. There are more than five times as many Democratic women as Republican women in the congressional pool of potential presidential candidates. This was reflected in the record number of women among the many Democrats vying to challenge President Donald Trump in the 2020 presidential elections. Among the six women who qualified for at least one of the Democratic debates, five were members of Congress. In contrast, the fact that women compose only 8 percent of the Republicans in Congress constrains the future possibilities for Republican women presidential candidates.

The partisan gap is reinforcing in other ways as well. Once in elective office, and particularly once in positions of leadership, women are more likely than men to prioritize recruiting women and be effective at recruiting women. Based on their interviews with most of the women in Congress, Dittmar, Sanbonmatsu, and Carroll found that "congresswomen take seriously their responsibility to serve as political role models for other women and share a commitment to increasing women's representation."[23] Studies suggest that men are less likely to recruit women—not because they are blatantly biased against women's candidacies but because they have fewer women in their social networks and are inclined to recruit people like themselves.[24] Commitment to recruiting and supporting women is something expressed by both Democratic and Republican women, but once again there are simply more women in the Democratic Party who are positioned to do this work and who have positions of leadership. This in turn has contributed to the widening of the partisan gap within state legislatures and has had reinforcing effects on party culture.

In addition to the short-term effects of women recruiting more women, there are longer-term effects of the partisan gap among women in elected office that also are likely to be reinforcing. The more the partisan gap grows, the more the Democratic Party appears as the natural home for women who seek political power. News coverage of high-profile Democratic women in elective office, such as Speaker Nancy Pelosi and the top women contenders for the 2020 Democratic presidential nomination, only reinforces the image of the Democratic Party as a welcome home for powerful women. Given research about the inspirational effects of women officeholders on young girls and women in the electorate,[25] it seems plausible that these high-profile Democrats may encourage a wider swath of young women Democrats to become interested in politics and consider a run for office.

Women in elected office see themselves as role models not only for girls but also for boys, changing the way Americans overall conceptualize those who hold political power and political office.[26] But what young people are seeing when they look at political coverage is many high-profile women Democrats and an almost exclusively white, male Republican Party. Thus, the partisan gap among women in elected office contributes to an even more dramatic gendering of the parties.[27] The growing gulf between the overwhelming white, male Republican

party-in-government and an increasingly diverse electorate may also have implications for the future viability of
the party. Some Republican party elites describe diversifying their party's elected officials in terms of gender as a
matter of party survival.[28]

The Partisan Gap and the Substantive
Representation of Democratic and Republican
Women in Congress

The partisan gap among women legislators at the state
and national levels also holds consequences for policy
representation. Past studies have examined the relationship between women's representation in legislative bodies
and policy outcomes. The consensus is that women's presence matters. Women bring distinctive life experiences, as
women, to their work as legislators, which infuses their
approach to working with their colleagues, agenda setting, and policy-making.[29] Although there is important
variation among women and across institutional contexts,
women in the aggregate prioritize different issues and
ensure issues relating to women get mainstreamed onto
the agenda more so than their men colleagues.[30] Greater
representation by women overall, and women of color in
particular, alters the deliberative processes, priorities, and
outcomes of political institutions.[31]

In the highly partisan environment of the twenty-first
century, what matters most in terms of understanding
women's substantive impact on policy is not the overall
number of women in elective office, but rather wom-
en's presence and power within their respective party
caucuses.[32] Reflecting the broader partisan polarization of American politics, the views of Democratic and

Republican women in society as well as in elective office are now far apart, shaped more by party than by gender.[33] Moreover, women are in the best position to influence policy when they are well represented in their parties, when they hold positions of leadership, and when their party is in power.

By these criteria, Democratic women are well positioned to meaningfully shape legislation and priorities in state legislatures and Congress. Women form 38 percent of Democrats in the US House of Representatives, 36 percent of Democrats in the US Senate, and 41 percent of Democratic state legislators nationally. Importantly, women of color are well represented among this group, forming 43 percent of Democratic women in Congress and 36 percent of Democratic women in state legislatures. This is crucial because women of color bring distinctive and diverse perspectives to their legislative work, shaped by their intersectional identities.[34]

Democratic women also hold key leadership positions, most notably the position of Speaker in the US House of Representatives, but also eleven other leadership roles in the US House and five leadership roles in the US Senate.[35] At the start of the 116th Congress, Democratic women chaired six committees in the House, including the powerful Appropriations Committee. Chairing congressional committees is important as chairs have significant power over the tone, agenda, strategy, and policy-making. On the state level, six Democratic women serve as speakers of state houses, and twelve Democratic women serve as presidents of state senates or as presidents pro tempore.[36] Through their strong numbers and leadership positions, this diverse group of women is well positioned to influence strategy, policy, and deliberation among Democrats.

While there are challenges with having a diverse coalition, perhaps highlighted most visibly in the tension between a group of young progressive women of color known as The Squad and Speaker of the House Nancy Pelosi over policy and party strategy, this diversity also enables the Democratic Party to anticipate and respond to the concerns of an increasingly diverse nation.

A number of excellent studies have documented the distinctive impact of Democratic women in office.[37] Building on these studies by exploring the impact of women in state legislatures where women are in the majority among the party in power holds potential for further insights. A brief look at the recent legislative sessions of Nevada and Colorado, two states where women form over 60 percent of Democrats in both chambers of the state legislatures, and where Democrats also hold the majority, offers some intriguing insights that should be investigated more fully. Nevada's biennial legislative session concluded in early June 2019 after passing seventeen bills related to issues disproportionately affecting women, including sex trafficking, sexual misconduct, equal pay, child marriage, and reproductive rights.[38] Similarly, Colorado's legislature made progress on bills relating to paid family leave, state funding for full-day kindergarten, and aggressive climate change legislation sponsored by four Democratic women.[39] Reporting also suggests that having women as a majority has shifted the culture of the work environments in both of the state houses.

Given that women only form 8 percent of Republicans in Congress, and only 17 percent of Republicans in state legislatures, their ability to shape policy is significantly less than that of their Democratic counterparts. Republican women are not only fewer in number than Democratic women, but they have less seniority, which further constrains their potential influence. When Republicans controlled the US House in the 115th Congress (2015–2017), only two Republican women led standing committees. Similarly, only two Republican women lead standing committees in the Republican-controlled US Senate in the 116th Congress (2019–2021). Republican women form less than one-fifth of Republicans in most state legislatures, hold many fewer leadership positions than their Democratic colleagues, and have especially low levels of representation in legislatures where their party is in power. As Republican-controlled legislatures and state governments, as well as Republican-controlled chambers of Congress, push for a range of policies, including policies disproportionately and/or differentially impacting women, women have a small seat at the table.

While the views of Republican women are not monolithic, there is a significant gender gap between the views of Republican men and Republican women in the electorate. Barnes and Cassese demonstrate that the views of Republican women are different than those of Republican men on a wide variety of issues, including ones traditionally considered women's issues such as abortion, childcare, education, and health policy, but also broader issues, including gay rights, taxes, and gun control.[40] Republican women in state legislatures also hold different views than their men colleagues.[41] As Dittmar, Sanbonmatsu, and Carroll document exhaustively in their book, *A Seat at the Table: Congresswomen's Perspectives on Why Their Presence Matters*,[42] and I found in my own interviews as well, Republican women in office believe strongly that they bring something unique to the legislative process and to policy deliberation. Given that Republican women have experiences, perspectives, and views that are different from those of Republican men, their dramatic underrepresentation in state legislatures and Congress is concerning.

One stark illustration of the marginalization, or rather absence, of Republican women's voices occurred in the 115th Congress. It was during these two years that the Republican-controlled US Senate considered President Trump's appointments to the Supreme Court, as well as a historic number of appointments to the federal judiciary. Supreme Court justices have enormous influence over policies that disproportionately affect women—issues ranging from abortion policy, to equal pay and employment discrimination, to health care. Moreover, President's Trump's nomination of Justice Brett Kavanaugh was highly controversial in part because Kavanaugh was accused of committing sexual assault when he was in high school. Despite the highly gendered implications of these judicial nominations, there were no Republican women on the Senate Judiciary Committee as it held hearings on them and only five Republican women in the Senate overall.[43] This means that as the Republican members of the Judiciary Committee discussed and crafted their strategy, conducted hearings, and deliberated over the nominations of Neil Gorsuch and Brett Kavanaugh, there were no women's voices among them. Given the distinctive way two of the five Republican women in the US Senate at the time responded to Kavanaugh's nomination—Susan Collins by expressing deep concern about the accusations against him, and Lisa Murkowski by failing to support his nomination—as well as President's Trump's derogatory comments about Kavanaugh's accuser,[44] it is possible that had Republican women had meaningful representation on the Senate Judiciary Committee the process would have unfolded differently. In contrast, four of the Democrats on the Senate Judiciary Committee were women, two women of color, and they used their positions on that committee to highlight women's distinctive perspectives and concerns.

The voices of Republican women were also absent as Republicans in the US Senate crafted their plan to repeal and replace Obamacare.[45] In the 115th Congress, Republican Senate majority leader Mitch McConnell appointed a fifteen-member panel to develop a Republican health care plan. As Michele Swers points out, "One group that was conspicuously absent from the appointed panel was Republican women."[46] Swers describes how the marginalization of women's voices among Senate Republicans as they crafted health care policy stood in stark contrast to the robust and meaningful role Democratic women in Congress had played in the development of the Affordable Care Act. Among other achievements, "Democratic women made sure that women could not be charged more than men and pregnancy, contraception, and maternity care were including among the essential health benefits that insurance plans must cover."[47]

The dramatic lack of women of color among Republicans in Congress and state legislatures holds policy consequences above and beyond the issues of marginalization just discussed. In the 116th Congress, there are no Republican women of color in the Senate and only one woman of color in the House of Representatives. Two Republican women of color left Congress in January 2019: Representative Mia Love, who was defeated in her quest for reelection, and Ileana Ros-Lehtinen, who retired after a long congressional career. In an interview reflecting on her career, Ros-Lehtinen suggested that the Republican Party in Congress had become too white and too male, and as a result was focusing too much on the issues of conservative white men at the expense of women and the Latinx community.[48] Along similar lines, Mia Love, the only Black Republican woman to have ever served in Congress, explained in an op-ed in the *Washington Post* how her experience as part of an immigrant family, who came to the United States from Haiti and prioritized hard work and giving back to the community, informed and strengthened her potential contributions as a legislator, particularly on immigration policy. She wrote that her own experience gave her "a unique perspective that can help facilitate immigration policy that works for everyone." Yet, she felt her perspective was not welcomed by her Republican colleagues. She wrote that "during my time in Congress, I never understood why I had to fight so hard to make my perspective heard on immigration."[49] The distinctive viewpoints of Republican women of color are significantly underrepresented, if not completely absent, in both chambers of Congress and state legislatures across the country.

The Partisan Gap and the Substantive Representation of Democratic and Republican Women in State Legislatures

The impact of the underrepresentation of Republican women can also be seen on the state level, highlighted here through a focus on two issues: reproductive rights and health care. State legislators have introduced, debated, and passed a large amount of pro-life/antichoice legislation in recent years, including "heartbeat bills" passed in Georgia, Missouri, and Louisiana. The states passing the most restrictive abortion laws have been those controlled by the Republican Party. What is sometimes overlooked, though, is that there are very few women among the Republicans introducing, debating, and voting on these policies. Women form, on average, only 16 percent of Republican legislators in the states that, according to the National Association for the Repeal of Abortion Laws (NARAL) Report Cards on Women's Reproductive Rights, have passed the most antichoice legislation in recent years. In regression analysis, not shown here, women's representation among Republican lawmakers is a strong, *inverse* predictor of more restrictive abortion policy. In other words, the fewer women there are among the Republican legislators, the more antichoice legislation the state has passed in recent years, a relationship that remains substantively strong and highly significant even when party control of the legislature is included in the model.[50] While the representation of women among Democratic lawmakers in these states is often robust, the minority party has little to no say in crafting such policies.

The most obvious implication is that policies having to do with the regulation of women's bodies and choices, and access to reproductive health care, are being introduced, debated, and passed with very few women's voices having input. This is particularly problematic because there is evidence that Republican women have different views on and approaches to this issue than their men colleagues. Even as Republican women state legislators have become more conservative over the past two decades, they remain significantly less conservative on the issue of abortion than their men counterparts.[51]

Additionally, studies show that even the growing number of very conservative, pro-life Republican women legislators at the state and national levels approach, frame, and craft pro-life policy in significantly different ways than their men colleagues.[52] In the spring of 2016, for example, several pro-life Republican women lawmakers in Indiana spoke out strongly against restrictive abortion legislation passed by their men colleagues and signed into law by then Republican governor Mike Pence, arguing it was too punitive toward women.[53] Another example can be seen in Oklahoma, where in spring 2016 the highly pro-life Republican governor, Mary Fallin, vetoed a law passed by her state's heavily Republican and heavily male legislature that would essentially ban abortions because she did not consider it a sensible approach to the issue. Once again, these Republican women are pro-life, but their approach to the issue is meaningfully different than that of their men colleagues.

On the flip side of the issue, it is interesting to note that Alaska, a state with a Republican-controlled legislature and one of the highest proportions of women among those Republicans, as well as two women in state legislative leadership positions, is rated by NARAL as having passed meaningful pro-choice legislation in recent years. Future research into the case of Alaska, both to understand why Republican women have achieved unusually high levels of representation in the state and to understand the specific role of Republican women in crafting and passing legislation would be instructive.

Another issue that highlights the substantive implications of so few Republican women in state legislatures can be seen in health care. One of the major provisions of the Affordable Care Act was the expansion of Medicaid eligibility to low-income adults. While this provision was intended to apply nationally, the Supreme Court ruling in 2012 made it optional for states. The decision about whether to expand Medicaid under Obamacare has been a highly politicized one, with states controlled by Democrats much more likely to expand Medicaid than Republican states. The decision is also a gendered one, in that it has a disproportionate impact on women. Women not only have different and often more serious health needs, but they are overrepresented among the group of low-income individuals who get covered in states that expand Medicaid; conversely, they are disproportionately among those without coverage in states that do not.[54] A comparison of means tests shows that women represented only 14 percent of Republican legislators in the states that decided not to expand Medicaid.[55] This is not to say that the outcome would be different if more Republican women were in these state legislatures, but rather to say that this decision, which disproportionately and differentially affects women, is being made without many Republican women offering their distinctive perspective.

Future Research on the Partisan Gap in Women's Representation

This book argues that four major developments in American electoral politics—the ideological, racial, and regional realignments of the parties, as well as the contrasting cultures of the parties—have contributed to the emergence and growth of the partisan gap among women in state legislatures and in Congress. A promising route for future research would be to engage these frameworks to explore the underrepresentation and partisan dynamics of women in other types of elective office, both in the United States and in comparative democracies.

One possibility would be to explore the case of women governors. Similar to women in state legislatures and Congress, the 2018 election was a particularly triumphant one for women governors. A record sixteen women ran for governor as major party nominees. In the wake of the 2018 election, nine women serve as governors. Three states—Maine, South Dakota, and Iowa—elected their first women governors. Despite these accomplishments, women remain significantly underrepresented among governors. Women are only 18 percent of the country's governors, which is lower than their levels of representation among state legislators and members of Congress.[56]

In several important ways, women's representation in governorships has not followed the same trajectory as their representation in state legislatures or Congress. There has not been a steady rise of Democratic women governors paired with stalled progress or a decline among Republican women governors. From 1980 to the present, there has been rough parity among women governors in the two parties: twenty-one Democratic women serving as governor and eighteen Republican women.[57] The overall number of women serving as governor at any one time has been small, but there have been a number of years when Republican women outnumbered Democratic women among governors.[58] Going into the 2018 elections, there were six women governors, and the majority, four of the six, were Republicans. Thus, the partisan gap has not been a driving force behind the underrepresentation of women governors as it has for women in other elective offices.

On the other hand, there are some signs that a structural advantage among Democratic women as governors may be emerging. From the 1980s to the present, the

Democratic Party has fielded significantly more women candidates for governor than the Republican Party, eighty-two to forty-five. The gap between Democratic and Republican women candidates has been especially large in the twenty-first century.[59] Similar to trends in Congress and state legislatures, there are fewer Republican women governors today than in the past. As of summer 2020 women hold six of the twenty-four governorships held by Democrats, or 25 percent. In contrast, women form just three of the twenty-six governorships held by Republicans, which is 12 percent.

The theoretical frameworks employed in this book may provide insights into why Democratic women have not amassed a consistent representational advantage over Republican women in governorships. One factor worth further study may be the few people of color, especially women of color, who have been elected governor. Indeed, women of color face their biggest challenges in terms of winning election to statewide office.[60] Given that the comparatively higher levels of representation among women of color compared with white women in state legislatures and Congress contribute to the partisan gap, the underrepresentation of women of color in statewide office helps to explain the lack of Democratic advantage among women governors. As women of color begin to make significant inroads into statewide elective office, however, it will most likely lead to a widening of the partisan gap among women governors. Relatedly, the robust and growing number of Democratic women in state legislatures, including the growing number of Democratic women legislators of color, creates a large and growing pool of potential gubernatorial candidates. It will be interesting to see if the current partisan gap among women governors persists or grows over the next several election cycles, and if so what role geography, race, ideology, and party culture play in these dynamics.

Another fruitful area to expand this research would be into local office. As with other elective offices, women are underrepresented in most elected positions in local government.[61] Melody Crowder-Meyer has done fascinating work in this area, finding that party officials at the local level engage in recruitment practices that disadvantage women, simply because most local officials are men and have mostly men in their networks.[62] Exploring the extent to which a partisan gap exists among women in local office, and the extent to which the ideological, racial, and regional polarization of the parties has contributed to these dynamics could yield important insights. Warshaw's review of research on local politics found that the ideological polarization of the parties plays a larger role in shaping local elections than previously thought.[63] The ideological polarization shaping so much else of contemporary electoral politics now shapes the behavior of local political officials as well. Building on this research to see how this ideological polarization has shaped the representation of women differentially by party would be instructive.

Finally, it would be useful to expand on research that explores the role of party in mediating women's representation, or lack thereof, in a comparative context. The relative underrepresentation of women in conservative parties is something found in other democracies around the world.[64] R. Campbell and Childs found that the Conservative Party in the United Kingdom, for example, has created a more challenging environment for women office seekers, by refusing to use quotas and stopping the use of other mechanisms to ensure descriptive representation of women even while claiming that it is interested in expanding women's representation.[65] Wineinger and Nugent's work represents an interesting step in this direction by explicitly comparing efforts by women within the Republican Party in the United States and the Conservative Party in the United Kingdom to navigate their parties' cultures and work toward the increased representation of women.[66] Tracing the emergence and expansion of the partisan gap among women in elected office in other democracies, paying particularly attention to the role of ideological polarization as well as the intersection of race, ethnicity, and gender may provide further insights.

The gap between women's representation in the Democratic and Republican parties, and in liberal versus conservative parties in democracies around the world, acts as a significant constraint on women's representation overall. Unless the Republican Party and other conservative parties are able to increase the representation of women among their officeholders, the possibility of gender parity in office will be very difficult, and most likely impossible, to achieve. On the other hand, women's steady progress among Democrats in the United States is encouraging, illustrating how democracy in the United States continues to become more reflective of its citizens. Tracking the partisan gap across future elections should provide further analytical insights, as well as examples of how democracy functions when women are proportionately represented among those in government.

ACKNOWLEDGMENTS

I first became fascinated with the large and growing gap between the number of Democratic women and Republican women in elective office—and with the causes and consequences of this overlooked partisan gap—in 2004, and I have been researching, presenting, and publishing on this topic ever since. I am grateful to NYU Press for giving me the opportunity to take my decades-long research passion and develop it into this book.

Even though it has been more than two decades since I completed my PhD in political science at The Ohio State University, this book owes a debt of gratitude to the professors with whom I worked closely while I was a graduate student there: Paul Allen Beck, the late William Nelson, Kira Sanbonmatsu, Katherine Tate, and Herb Weisberg. Their courses, mentoring, and research have had a profound impact on my work as a political science professor and scholar, and on this project in particular.

This book very much stands on the shoulders of these giants in the discipline of political science and many other exceptional scholars whose work I drew on to construct the driving argument of this book, that the profound changes in American electoral politics—the ideological, regional, and racial realignment of the two major parties—have had significant and largely overlooked consequences for women in elective office, driving the chasmic partisan gap we see today, with Democratic women forming more than 80 percent of the women in Congress.

There are so many fellow political scientists who have been kinder and more generous than was necessary as I worked on this research project over the years: providing helpful feedback, writing letters of support, giving me opportunities to present my findings, sharing their expertise, and offering kind words to let me know my research was indeed valuable. Among the many I owe a great debt of gratitude are Nadia Brown, Barbara Burrell, Stefanie Chambers, Rosalyn Cooperman, Melody Crowder-Meyer, Melissa Deckman, Kelly Dittmar, Brian Frederick, Steven Greene, Farida Jalalzai, Mary-Kate Lizotte, Lanethea Mathews-Schultz, Malliga Och, Zoe Oxley, Dante Scala, Becki Scola, Shauna Shames, Michele Swers, Danielle Thomsen, Catherine Wineinger, and Christina Wolbrecht.

I have been a professor of political science at Hartwick College in Oneonta, New York, since the fall of 1999. At Hartwick I have had the privilege to help promote civil dialogue on important political issues, as well as foster informed and engaged citizenship through teaching a range of courses on American politics. Hartwick College has also provided me with pivotal support for my research endeavors. This project benefited directly from two Hartwick College Faculty Research Grants, one that allowed me to travel to Washington, DC, to conduct interviews and one that allowed me to hire a summer research assistant. Thank you to Abby Meltzer '20 for her absolutely outstanding research support during the summer of 2019, which was crucial to the timely completion of this book and the high quality of the data in the empirical chapters.

I owe a huge thank-you to my former student and Hartwick graduate Jon Taets '02, who drew on his expansive

Capitol Hill network to help me set up interviews with party officials, members of Congress and their staffs, and leaders among those seeking to recruit women candidates. Jon took my Parties and Elections class in the fall of 2000, the first time I ever taught the course; fourteen years later he was my teacher and guide as he showed me around the real world of party politics on Capitol Hill.

Thank you also to my friend Susan Young and her sister Amy Young, who drew on her expansive Washington, DC, network to help me set up a number of pivotal interviews that yielded important insights into my research topic.

I express profound gratitude to all who sat for interviews with me: this includes party and organizational elites, including women members of Congress, women candidates, high-level congressional staffers and campaign workers, current and former members of the parties' congressional campaign and national committees, and high-level individuals working for organizations committed to recruiting and/or supporting women's candidacies. These interviews provided invaluable insights into the role of the national parties as well as nonparty organizations in recruiting and supporting women candidates. All of these individuals were generous with their time and knowledge, typically going well beyond the specific time scheduled for our interviews. Insights from those who actually "do politics" rather than just study politics make this a much better and more insightful book.

A sincere thank-you to Shauna Shames and Political Parity, a nonpartisan organization committed to increasing women's representation in elective office, for sharing with me the key findings from additional in-depth interviews with Republican elites, including women members of Congress.

I am indebted to the Center for American Women and Politics and the National Conference of State Legislatures. Both of these organizations collect and make public a tremendous amount of information about gender, partisanship, and office holding in the United States. Data from these two sources were absolutely essential to the analyses presented in this book.

I offer my sincere gratitude to my editor at NYU Press, Sonia Tsuruoka. Sonia had great confidence in this project from its inception through its publication. Having such a supportive person guide me through the challenging process of writing, revising, and preparing a book for publication made what could have been a frustrating process into an enjoyable one. Thank you also to the anonymous reviewers of the manuscript, each of whom offered keen insights and suggestions about how to strengthen the book, as well as very welcome enthusiasm for the project. Their knowledgeable, constructive suggestions played a profound role in the final structure of the book and, without a doubt, made it so much better.

I conclude with a note of thanks to all the women who run for elective office in the United States. I began this research project because I believe our democracy would be even stronger and healthier if our elected officials more fully reflected the nation in terms of gender, race, and ethnicity. Running for elective office and serving in public office require incredible time and sacrifice. I am profoundly grateful to all who are willing to take on this challenge and help move the United States toward a more perfect union.

NOTES

INTRODUCTION

1 See Atkeson and Carrillo 2007; D. E. Campbell and Wolbrecht 2006; Elder 2004; Mansbridge 1999.

2 See Anzia and Berry 2011; Carroll 2001b; Dodson 2001; Pearson and Dancey 2011; Swers 2002, 2013, 2016; Thomas 1994; Volden, Wiseman, and Wittmer 2013.

3 See Dittmar, Sanbonmatsu, and Carroll 2018; Thomsen 2013.

4 CAWP 2020g.

5 CAWP 2020e.

6 This figure is accurate as of summer 2020.

7 See CAWP 2020d.

8 Chambers and Elder 2020.

9 Dittmar 2019.

10 CAWP 2020f.

11 NCSL 2020a.

12 CAWP 2020a.

13 NCSL 2020a.

14 CAWP. 2020d.

15 Kaufmann 2006; Kaufmann and Petrocik 1999.

16 Bureau of Labor Statistics 2017.

17 Council of Economic Advisers 2014.

18 Darcy, Welch, and Clark 1994.

19 Schreiber 2014.

20 Deckman 2016, 2–3.

21 Storey 2016.

22 Jacobson 2015.

23 Elder 2004; Lawless and Fox 2010.

24 Burrell 1996.

25 Darcy, Welch, and Clark 1994.

26 E.g., Burrell 1996; Niven 1998, 2006; Sanbonmatsu 2006.

27 Lawless and Fox 2018.

28 Jardina 2019a, 2019b.

29 Abramson 2019; Connolly 2018.

30 Abramowitz 2018; J. E. Campbell 2016.

31 Pew Research Center 2014.

32 Norrander and Wilcox 2005; Palmer and Simon 2006; Sanbon-matsu 2006.

33 Elder and Greene 2012, chap. 3; Freeman 1993, 1997, 1999; Wolbrecht 2000.

34 Elder and Greene 2012, chap. 3.

35 Klinkner and Schaller 2006.

36 R. Fox 2018; Norrander and Wilcox 2014; Palmer and Simon 2006.

37 Carmines and Stimson 1989.

38 Crowder-Meyer and Cooperman 2018; Freeman 1986; Grossman and Hopkins 2016, 2015; Wineinger 2018.

39 Burrell 2014; Maestas, Maisel, and Stone 2005; Sanbonmatsu 2006.

40 Carroll and Sanbonmatsu 2013; Lawless and Fox 2010.

41 Scola 2013, 2014.

42 Burrell 2014.

43 Och 2018.

44 Sanbonmatsu 2006.

45 Och 2018, 17.

46 Atkeson and Carrillo 2007; Elder 2004.

47 Dittmar, Sanbonmatsu, and Carroll 2018; Swers 2013, 2016; Wineinger 2018, 2019.

48 Barnes and Cassese 2017; Carroll and Sanbonmatsu 2013.

49 Abramson 2019.

1. A TALE OF TWO PARTIES

1 Abramowitz 2018; J. E. Campbell 2016.

2 Pew Research Center 2014.

3 Pew Research Center 2014.

4 Barber and McCarty 2013.

5 Grossman and Hopkins 2015, 2016.

6 Abramowitz 2018.

7 Hetherington and Weiler 2018.

 8 Bishop 2009.
 9 Elazar 1984; Norrander and Wilcox 2005; Palmer and Simon 2006.
10 Hogan 2001; Norrander and Wilcox 2005; Palmer and Simon 2006.
11 Thomsen 2014, 2015.
12 Carroll and Sanbonmatsu 2013, 92.
13 A. R. Hunt 2014.
14 Matland and King 2006.
15 Wolbrecht 2000.
16 Freeman 1993; Grossman and Hopkins 2016.
17 Swers and Larson 2005.
18 Burrell 2018; Elder and Greene 2012, chap. 3.
19 Elder, Greene, and Lizotte forthcoming; Swers and Larson 2005; Wolbrecht 2000.
20 Freeman 1993, 1999; Wolbrecht 2000.
21 Sanbonmatsu 2004.
22 Elder and Greene 2012, chap. 3.
23 Swers and Larson 2005, 124.
24 Burrell 2018, 225; Och 2018, 14–15.
25 ABC News/Fusion Poll 2013.
26 Cooper et al. 2016.
27 Elder and Greene 2016; Pew Research Center 2013.
28 Elder and Greene 2016; Elder, Greene, and Lizotte forthcoming.
29 Norrander and Wilcox 2014, 187.
30 Hicks et al. 2018; Klinkner and Schaller 2006; Petrocik 1987.
31 Petrocik 1987.
32 Klinkner and Schaller 2006, 6.
33 Bullock, Hoffman, and Gaddie 2006; Klinkner and Schaller 2006.
34 Brewer, Mariani, and Stonecash 2002.
35 Norrander and Wilcox 2005; R. Fox 2018; O'Regan and Stambough 2014.
36 Elazar 1984; Hill 1981.
37 Burrell 1996; Norrander and Wilcox 2005; O'Regan and Stambough 2014.
38 Darcy, Welch, and Clark 1994; Ondercin and Welch 2005; O'Regan and Stambough 2014; Palmer and Simon 2006.

39 Crenshaw 1989; see also Cho, Crenshaw, and McCall 2013; Simien 2007; Smooth 2013.

40 Tate 1994.

41 Tate 1994, 1997.

42 Hicks et al. 2018.

43 Smooth 2018.

44 Congressional Research Service 2020, 7. Following the Congressional Research Service coding system, members of Congress who identify as belonging to multiple racial and ethnic minority groups are counted for each group. For example, Kamala Harris is counted as both Black American and Asian American.

45 Hicks et al. 2018, 409.

46 Elder 2008; Scola 2013, 2014.

47 Bejarano 2013; Garcia Bedolla, Tate, and Wong 2014; Tate 1997.

48 Bejarano 2013; Brown and Dowe 2020.

49 Gertzog 2002, 108–110; Smooth 2006; Tate 2003, 60–64.

50 Brown and Dowe 2020; Chambers and Elder 2020; Dittmar 2019.

51 Chambers and Elder 2020; Elder and Frederick 2019; Simien 2015.

52 Philpot and Walton 2007.

53 Bejarano 2013.

54 Brown and Dowe 2020.

55 Abramowitz 2018; Abramowitz and McCoy 2019; Carmines and Stimson 1989; Key 1949.

56 Abramowitz and McCoy 2019.

57 Hetherington, Long, and Rudolph 2016, 321.

58 Wong 2019.

59 Jardina 2019b; Junn 2017; Strolovitch, Wong, and Proctor 2017.

60 Abramowitz and McCoy 2019.

61 Hooghe and Dassonneville 2018.

62 Jardina 2019a.

63 Aldrich 1995.

64 Burrell 2018; Maestas, Maisel, and Stone 2005.

65 Burrell 2018.

66 Desmarais, La Raja, and Kowal 2015; Koger, Masket, and Noel 2009.

67 Lawless and Fox 2010, 2018.

68 Carroll and Sanbonmatsu 2013.

69 Drusch 2014.

70 Burrell 1996, 2018.

71 Burrell 2018; Crowder-Meyer and Cooperman 2018.

72 Freeman 1986; Grossman and Hopkins 2015, 2016.

73 Freeman 1986.

74 Och 2018; see also Cooperman and Crowder-Meyer 2018; Wineinger 2018.

75 Freeman 1986.

76 Crowder-Meyer 2013; Sanbonmatsu 2006.

2. THE GROWING CHASM

1 NCSL 2020c.

2 Fadel 2019.

3 Elder 2008; Maestas, Maisel, and Stone 2005.

4 CAWP 2020f.

5 CAWP 2020f.

6 Paxton, Painter, and Hughes 2009.

7 Heldman and Wade 2011, 156.

8 Norrander and Wilcox 2014, 280.

9 Figure 2.1 was calculated by the author using data from CAWP and NCSL. This and the other figures in the book use data current as of August 2019 unless otherwise noted.

10 Storey 2016.

11 Paxton, Painter, and Hughes 2009.

12 Heldman and Wade 2011.

13 Norrander and Wilcox 2005, 2014.

14 Elder 2012, 2014a, 2014b.

15 Thomsen 2015; Carroll and Sanbonmatsu 2013.

16 Elazar 1984; Norrander and Wilcox 2014, 2005; Ransford, Hardy-Fanta, and Cammisa 2007, 29–30.

17 Darcy, Welch, and Clark 1994.

18 Mayhew 1986; Norrander and Wilcox 2014, 275.

19 Arceneaux 2001; Norrander and Wilcox 2014; Sanbonmatsu 2006, 2018.

20 Klinkner and Schaller 2006.

21 Thomas 1994.

22 Childs and Krook 2006; Grey 2006, 494. For a fuller discussion of the controversies surrounding the concept of critical mass,

see the roundtable of articles in "Do Women Represent Women? Rethinking the 'Critical Mass' Debate," *Politics & Gender* 2, no. 4 (December 2006): 492–530.

23 E.g., Brown 2014; Dittmar, Sanbonmatsu, and Carroll 2018; Mansbridge 1999.

24 Fadel 2019.

25 Barnes and Cassese 2017; Carroll and Sanbonmatsu 2013.

26 Elder 2012; Niven 2006; Stambough and O'Regan 2007.

27 NCSL 2020a.

28 Elazar 1984.

29 According to state ideology data originally collected by Berry et al. (1998) and updated by Fording (2018), the only two Republican-controlled states that are less conservative are Florida and Iowa.

30 NCSL 2020a, 2020b.

31 Storey 2016.

32 NCSL 2020b.

33 Norrander and Wilcox 2014, 279.

34 Arceneaux 2001.

35 Klinkner and Schaller 2006.

36 Norrander and Wilcox 2014.

37 Elder 2014b.

38 Kurtz 2015; Reingold 2019, 426.

39 Casellas 2011; Kurtz 2015.

40 Casellas 2011; Hicks et al. 2018.

41 Hicks et al. 2018; Kurtz 2015.

42 Casellas 2011; Hicks et al. 2018; Kurtz 2015; Preuhs and Juenke 2011.

43 Kurtz 2015; McKee and Springer 2015.

44 Reingold 2019.

45 Brown 2014; Smooth 2018.

46 Bejarano 2013; Chambers and Elder 2020; Philpot and Walton 2007; Simien 2015; Stokes-Brown and Dolan 2010.

47 Scola 2014, 12.

48 Kurtz 2015.

49 Kurtz 2015; McKee and Springer 2015.

50 Kurtz 2015.

51 CAWP 2020a; NALEO 2018.

52 CAWP 2020a.

53 CAWP 2020a, 2020f.

54 Statistics calculated by author using data from CAWP 2020a and NCSL 2020b.

55 NCSL 2020b.

56 Hicks et al. 2018.

57 Casellas 2011.

58 The measure for this comes from Berry et al. (1998) and is updated through 2016 by Fording (2018).

59 E.g., Elder 2008, 2014a; Norrander and Wilcox 2005; Rule 1999; Sanbonmatsu 2002.

60 Bureau of Labor Statistics 2017.

61 Bureau of Labor Statistics 2017.

62 Sanbonmatsu 2006.

63 Norrander and Wilcox 2014, 187.

64 Scola 2014.

65 Darcy, Welch, and Clark 1994.

66 Darcy, Welch, and Clark 1994; Reingold 2019.

67 Williams 2018.

68 States with multimember districts are coded as 1, and as 0 otherwise.

69 Williams 2018.

70 Carroll and Sanbonmatsu 2013; Sanbonmatsu 2006.

71 Sanbonmatsu 2002, 2006.

72 Norrander and Wilcox 2014.

73 Carroll and Sanbonmatsu 2013, 92.

74 Party organization strength is based on David Mayhew's Traditional Party Organization (TPO) scores, which range from 1 to 5, where 5 is the strongest. This measure is based on organizational strength, including influence over nominations (Mayhew 1986, 196). This measure of party organizational strength has been employed in a number of other studies of women's representation in state legislatures, including Sanbonmatsu 2006; Elder 2012, 2018.

75 Sanbonmatsu 2002.

76 Brown and Dowe 2020.

77 Sanbonmatsu 2006, 73.

78 Crowder-Meyer 2013; Niven 1998, 2006; Sanbonmatsu 2006.

79 CAWP 2018.

80 Bradshaw and Cooperman 2011.

81 NCSL 2015.

82 Arceneaux 2001; Carroll and Jenkins 2001, 2005; Paxton, Painter, and Hughes 2009.

83 O'Regan and Stambough 2018.

84 Sanbonmatsu 2015.

3. WHITHER REPUBLICAN WOMEN?

1 Dittmar 2019.

2 Dittmar 2019.

3 CAWP. 2020a.

4 CAWP 2020a.

5 Darcy, Welch, and Clark 1994.

6 Elder 2004; Lawless and Fox 2010.

7 E.g., Burrell 1996; Kittilson and Fridkin 2008.

8 Klinkner and Schaller 2006.

9 Bullock, Hoffman, and Gaddie 2006; Klinkner and Schaller 2006.

10 The geographic regions in table 3.1 are the same as those used in chapter 2 and are based on the regional classifications used by Klinkner and Schaller (2006) in their assessment of regional partisan realignments.

11 Fox 2014.

12 Palmer and Simon 2006.

13 Congressional Research Service 2020.

14 All data are from Congress Research Service 2020. Some members identify as belonging to two races and therefore are counted two times in these statistics. Nonvoting delegates are not included.

15 Garcia Bedolla, Tate, and Wong 2014.

16 Congressional Research Service 2020.

17 Tate 1997.

18 Gershon 2012; Ward 2016.

19 Gertzog 2002, 108–110; Smooth 2006; Tate 2003, 60–64.

20 Lublin 2018.

21 Brown and Dowe 2020; Garcia Bedolla, Tate, and Wong 2014; Philpot and Walton 2007; Tate 1997.

22 Chambers and Elder 2020; Simien 2015; Elder and Frederick 2019.

23 Philpot and Walton 2007.

24 Lublin 2018.

25 Congressional Research Service 2020, 5.

26 Fry 2019.

27 Darcy, Welch, and Clark 1994.

28 Rowe 2018.

29 Palmer and Simon 2006, 196.

30 Bird 2006; Maestas, Maisel, and Stone 2005.

31 NCSL 2019b.

32 In the 116th Congress, 24 Republicans and 22 Democrats serving in the Senate have state legislative experience; 106 Democrats and 89 Republicans in the House have state legislative experience.

33 Elder 2008.

34 Silva and Skulley 2019.

35 Garcia Bedolla, Tate, and Wong 2014.

4. LEFT OUT OF THE PARTY

1 Carroll and Sanbonmatsu 2013; Lawless and Fox 2010.

2 Crowder-Meyer and Cooperman 2018; Freeman 1986; Grossman and Hopkins 2015, 2016.

3 Aldrich 1995; Burrell 2014; Maestas, Maisel, and Stone 2005.

4 Desmarais, La Raja, and Kowal 2015; Koger, Masket, and Noel 2009.

5 Burrell 2018.

6 Carroll and Sanbonmatsu 2013; Lawless and Fox 2010.

7 Burrell 1996, 2014.

8 Burrell 2018; E. Johnson 2017.

9 Crowder-Meyer and Cooperman 2018.

10 Freeman 1986.

11 Grossman and Hopkins 2015, 119.

12 Cooperman and Crowder-Meyer 2018, 111.

13 Freeman 1986, 1993, 1997, 1999.

14 Cooper et al. 2016.

15 Burrell 2014.

16 O'Keefe 2012.

17 Bowman 2016.

18 Gonzalez-Ramirez 2019.

19 Niven 1998; Sanbonmatsu 2006.

20 Pathe 2016.

21 Freeman 1986.

22 Burrell 2014.

23 Pathe 2016.

24 Beckwith 2013; O'Keefe 2012.

25 Sarasohn 2013.

26 Burrell 2014; Nagourney and Zernike 2006.

27 Burrell 2014.

28 Fraga and Hassell 2020.

29 Dayen 2018; Hook 2014.

30 Chambers and Elder 2020.

31 Dittmar 2019.

32 Brown and Dowe 2020.

33 S. Johnson 2013.

34 Burrell 2018.

35 Burrell 2018, 239.

36 Cooperman and Crowder-Meyer 2018, 109; Crowder-Meyer and Cooperman 2018.

37 Jones 2019.

38 Dittmar 2015, 762.

39 A. R. Hunt 2014.

40 Cooperman and Crowder-Meyer 2018; Crowder-Meyer and Cooperman 2018.

41 Kitchens and Swers 2016; Thomsen and Swers 2017.

42 Burrell 2018.

43 Burrell 2014.

44 E.g., Chavez 2019.

45 Burrell 2006.

46 Blake 2007.

47 Burrell 2014; Rosin 2014.

48 Och 2018; Wineinger 2018.

49 Freeman 1986; Grossman and Hopkins 2016.

50 Cooperman and Crowder-Meyer 2018, 111; Freeman 1986, 332.

51 Och 2018.

52 Mimms 2013.

53 Henderson and Kucinich 2014.

54 Astor 2019.

55 Abramson 2019.

56 Day 2014; Republican National Committee 2013.

57 Cooperman and Crowder-Meyer 2018; Wineinger 2018.

58 Railey 2014.

59 Pathe 2018.

60 Och 2018.

61 Och 2018, 10.

62 Burrell 2018.

63 Puglise 2015.

64 Trygstad 2010.

65 Burrell 2018.

66 Mimms 2013.

67 Haberman, Martin, and Fandos 2020.

68 CAWP 2020g.

69 Lynch 2017.

70 CAWP 2020g.

71 Haberman, Martin, and Fandos 2020.

72 Newton-Small 2014b.

73 Newton-Small 2014a.

74 Dolan 2003.

75 Carroll and Sanbonmatsu 2013.

76 Abramson 2019.

77 Dittmar, Sanbonmatsu, and Carroll 2018.

78 Schuller 2019.

79 Brufke 2019.

80 Pathe 2018.

81 Shames 2018.

82 Kitchens and Swers 2016.

83 Abramson 2019.

84 Pathe 2018.

85 Livingston 2014.

86 Pathe 2019.

87 Abramson 2019.

88 Pathe 2018.

89 Abramson 2019.

90 Burrell 2018.

91 Astor 2019; NBC 2019.
92 Och 2018, 7.
93 Burrell 2018, 242.
94 Astor 2019.
95 Crowder-Meyer and Cooperman 2018.
96 Burrell 2018, 243.
97 Burrell 2006, 154–155.

CONCLUSION

1 Burrell 2018.
2 Lawless and Fox 2018.
3 Dittmar 2019.
4 Jacobson 2019.
5 Strolovitch, Wong, and Proctor 2017.
6 DiSalvo 2012; Dowe 2016.
7 Frymer 1999.
8 Abramowitz 2018; Abramowitz and McCoy 2019; Jardina 2019a.
9 Hicks et al. 2018; Lublin 2018.
10 Dittmar 2019.
11 Frymer 1999.
12 Kawashima-Ginsberg 2018.
13 NBC 2019.
14 Cornwell 2019.
15 CAWP 2020c; Zhou 2020.
16 Astor 2019; NBC 2019; Zhou 2020.
17 Freeman 1986; Grossman and Hopkins 2015, 2016; Crowder-Meyer and Cooperman 2018; Och 2018; Wineinger 2018.
18 Benen 2019.
19 Benen 2019.
20 Dittmar, Sanbonmatsu, and Carroll 2018.
21 Burrell 1996; Gertzog 2002.
22 As of September 2020, there were 670 Republican women state legislators, and in 1995 there were 673 (NCSL 2020c).
23 Dittmar, Sanbonmatsu, and Carroll 2018, 3.
24 Crowder-Meyer 2013; Niven 1998; Sanbonmatsu 2006.
25 Atkeson and Carrillo 2007, D. E. Campbell and Wolbrecht 2006; Elder 2004.
26 Dittmar, Sanbonmatsu, and Carroll 2018.

27 Winter 2010.
28 Abramson 2019; Connolly 2018.
29 Dittmar, Sanbonmatsu, and Carroll 2018.
30 Dodson 2001; Swers 2002, 2013; Thomas 1994.
31 E.g., Brown 2014; Dowe 2016; Garcia Bedolla, Tate, and Wong 2014; Mansbridge 1999.
32 Osborn 2012; Osborn and Kreitzer 2014; Swers 2014, 2018.
33 Barnes and Cassese 2017; Carroll and Sanbonmatsu 2013; Frederick 2013, 2011.
34 Bratton, Haynie, and Reingold 2006; Brown 2014; Garcia Bedolla, Tate, and Wong 2014; Gay and Tate 1998.
35 CAWP 2020d.
36 NCSL 2020a.
37 E.g., Osborne 2012; Swers 2002, 2013, 2014.
38 CBS News 2019; S. Hunt 2019.
39 Tumulty 2019.
40 Barnes and Cassese 2017.
41 Carroll and Sanbonmatsu 2013, 81.
42 Dittmar, Sanbonmatsu, and Carroll 2018.
43 Michele Swers (2013, 2018) points out that Republican leadership had been trying to recruit one of the party's few women members to serve on the Senate Judiciary Committee but had been unsuccessful. In the 116th Congress, however, two Republican women serve on the Senate Judiciary, Marcia Blackburn and Joni Ernst.
44 Baker and Fandos 2018.
45 Pear 2017.
46 Swers 2018, 200.
47 Swers 2018, 200.
48 NPR 2018.
49 Love 2018.
50 Elder 2018.
51 Carroll and Sanbonmatsu 2013, 79–81.
52 Reingold et al. 2015; Swers 2018.
53 Mosbergen 2016.
54 American College of Obstetricians and Gynecologists 2013; Ranji, Bair, and Salganicoff 2016.
55 Elder 2018.

56 CAWP 2020e.
57 CAWP 2020b.
58 O'Regan and Stambough 2014.
59 CAWP 2020c.
60 Dittmar 2019.
61 Holman 2019.
62 Crowder-Meyer 2013.
63 Warshaw 2019.
64 Och 2018.
65 R. Campbell and Childs 2015.
66 Wineinger and Nugent 2020.

BIBLIOGRAPHY

ABC News/Fusion Poll. 2013. "Poll Finds Vast Gaps in Basic Views on Gender, Race, Religion and Politics." October 28. www.langerre search.com.

Abramowitz, Alan I. 2018. *The Great Alignment: Race, Party Trans-formation, and the Rise of Donald Trump*. New Haven, CT: Yale University Press.

Abramowitz, Alan, and Jennifer McCoy. 2019. "United States: Racial Resentment, Negative Partisanship, and Polarization in Trump's America." *ANNALS of the American Academy of Political and Social Science* 681 (1): 137–156.

Abramson, Alana. 2019. "Congresswoman Elise Stefanik Has a Plan to Get More Republican Congresswomen Elected." *Time*, May 9. www.time.com.

Aldrich, John. 1995. *Why Parties? The Origin and Transformation of Political Parties in America*. Chicago: University of Chicago Press.

American College of Obstetricians and Gynecologists. 2013. "Ben-efits to Women of Medicaid Expansion through the Affordable Care Act. Committee Opinion No. 552." *Obstetrics & Gynecology* 121:223–225. www.acog.org.

Anzia, Sarah F., and Christopher R. Berry. 2011. "The Jackie (and Jill) Robinson Effect: Why Do Congresswomen Outperform Congress-men?" *American Journal of Political Science* 55 (3): 478–493.

Arceneaux, Kevin. 2001. "The 'Gender Gap' in State Legislative Repre-sentation: New Data to Tackle an Old Question." *Political Research Quarterly* 54 (1): 143–161.

Astor, Maggie. 2019. "'It Can't Be Worse': How Republican Women Are Trying to Rebuild." *New York Times*, July 9. www.nytimes.com.

Atkeson, Lonna Rae, and Nancy Carrillo. 2007. "More Is Better: The Influence of Collective Female Descriptive Representation on External Efficacy." *Politics & Gender* 3 (1): 79–101.

Baker, Peter, and Nicholas Fandos. 2018. "Trump Unleashes on Kavanaugh Accuser as Key Republican Wavers." *New York Times*, September 25. www.nytimes.com.

Barber, Michael, and Nolan McCarty. 2013. "Causes and Consequences of Polarization." In *Negotiating Agreement in Politics: Report of the Task Force on Negotiating Agreement in Politics*, edited by Jane Mansbridge and C. J. Martin, 19–53. Washington, DC: American Political Science Association.

Barnes, Tiffany D., and Erin C. Cassese. 2017. "American Party Women: A Look at the Gender Gap within Parties." *Political Research Quarterly* 70 (1): 127–141. doi:10.1177/1065912916675738.

Beckwith, Karen. 2013, "The Widening Partisan Gender Gap in the U.S. Congress." *Scholars Strategy Network*, March 1. www.scholars .org.

Bejarano, Christina E. 2013. *The Latina Advantage: Gender, Race, and Political Success*. Austin: University of Texas Press.

Benen, Steve. 2019. "GOP Leader: Pelosi Bears Responsibility for Party's Lack of Diversity." MSNBC, January 21. www.msnbc.com.

Berry, William D., Evan J. Ringquist, Richard C. Fording, and Russell L. Hanson. 1998. "Measuring Citizen and Government Ideology in the American States, 1960–93." *American Journal of Political Science* 42 (1): 327–348.

Bird, Michael. 2006. "Marching Off to Congress." *State Legislatures Magazine*, December, 16.

Bishop, Bill. 2009. *The Big Sort: Why the Clustering of Like-Minded America Is Tearing Us Apart*. Boston: Mariner Books.

Blake, Aaron. 2007. "House Republicans Aim for More Recruitment of Women in 2008." *The Hill*, January 23. www.thehill.com.

The Book of the States. 1975–2007. The Council of State Governments.

Bowman, Bridget. 2016. "Female Democrats Work to Boost Senate Ranks." *Roll Call*, October 13. www.rollcall.com.

Bradshaw, Samantha, and Rosalynn Cooperman. 2011. "Where Are the Women? Women as Candidates in the Republican Party of Virginia." *Virginia Social Science Journal* 46:19–38.

Bratton, Kathleen A., Kerry L. Haynie, and Beth Reingold. 2006. "Agenda Setting and African American Women in State Legislatures." *Journal of Women, Politics & Policy* 28 (3–4): 71–96.

Brewer, Mark D., Mack D. Mariani, and Jeffrey M. Stonecash. 2002. "Northern Democrats and Party Polarization in the US House." *Legislative Studies Quarterly* 27 (3): 423–444.

Brown, Nadia E. 2014. *Sisters in the Statehouse: Black Women and Legislative Decision Making.* Oxford: Oxford University Press.

Brown, Nadia E., and Pearl K. Dowe. 2020. "Late to the Party: Black Women's Inconsistent Support from Political Parties." In *Good Reasons to Run: Women and Political Candidacy*, edited by Shauna L. Shames, Rachel I. Bernhard, Mirya R. Holman, and Dawn Langan Teele, 153–166. Philadelphia: Temple University Press.

Brufke, Juliegrace. 2019. "GOP Amps Up Efforts to Recruit Women Candidates." *The Hill*, May 25. www.thehill.com.

Bullock, Charles S., Donna R. Hoffman, and Ronald Keith Gaddie. 2006. "Regional Variations in the Realignment of American Politics, 1944–2004." *Social Science Quarterly* 87 (3): 494–518.

Bureau of Labor Statistics. 2017. "Women in the Labor Force: A Data Book." United States Department of Labor. www.bls.gov.

Burrell, Barbara. 1996. *A Woman's Place Is in the House: Campaigning for Congress in the Feminist Era.* Ann Arbor: University of Michigan Press.

———. 2006. "Political Parties and Women's Organizations: Bringing Women into the Electoral Arena." In *Gender and Elections: Shaping the Future of American Politics*, edited by Susan J. Carroll and Richard L. Fox, 143–168. New York: Cambridge University Press.

———. 2014. "Political Parties and Women's Organizations: Bringing Women into the Electoral Arena." In *Gender and Elections: Shaping the Future of American Politics*, 3rd ed., edited by Susan J. Carroll and Richard L. Fox, 211–240. New York: Cambridge University Press.

———. 2018. "Political Parties and Women's Organizations: Bringing Women into the Electoral Arena." In *Gender and Elections: Shaping the Future of American Politics*, 4th ed., edited by Susan J. Carroll and Richard L. Fox, 220–249. New York: Cambridge University Press.

Campbell, David E., and Christina Wolbrecht. 2006. "See Jane Run: Women Politicians as Role Models for Adolescents." *American Journal of Political Science* 68 (2): 233–247.

Campbell, James E. 2016. *Polarized: Making Sense of a Divided America.* Princeton, NJ: Princeton University Press.

Campbell, Rosie, and Sarah Childs. 2015. "Conservatism, Feminization, and the Representation of Women in UK Politics." *British
Politics* 10 (2): 148–168.

Carmines, Edward G., and James S. Stimson. 1989. *Issue Evolution:
Race and the Transformation of American Politics*. Princeton, NJ:
Princeton University Press.

Carroll, Susan J. 2001a. "The Impact of Term Limits on Women." *Spectrum: The Journal of State Government* 74 (Fall): 19–21.

———. 2001b. "Representing Women: Women State Legislators as
Agents of Policy-Related Change." In *The Impact of Women in
Public Office*, edited by Susan J. Carroll, 3–21. Bloomington: Indi-
ana University Press.

———. 2002. "Partisan Dynamics of the Gender Gap among State
Legislators." *Spectrum: The Journal of State Government* 75 (Fall):
18–21.

Carroll, Susan, and Krista Jenkins. 2001. "Unrealized Opportunity?
Term Limits and the Representation of Women in State Legislatures." *Women & Politics* 23 (4): 1–30.

———. 2005. "Increasing Diversity or More of the Same? Term Limits
and the Representation of Women, Minorities, and Minority
Women in State Legislatures." *National Political Science Review*
10:71–84.

Carroll, Susan J., and Kira Sanbonmatsu. 2013. *More Women Can Run:
Gender and Pathways to the State Legislatures*. New York: Oxford
University Press.

Casellas, Jason P. 2011. *Latino Representation in State Houses and Congress*. New York: Cambridge University Press.

CBS News. 2019. "First Majority-Female Legislature Pushing for
Change in Nevada." June 1. www.cbsnews.com.

Center for American Women and Politics (CAWP). 2018. "Women in
State Legislatures 2018." Center for American Women in Politics.
www.cawp.rutgers.edu.

———. 2020a. "Facts on Women of Color in Office." Center for American Women in Politics. www.cawp.rutgers.edu.

———. 2020b. "History of Women Governors." Center for American
Women in Politics. www.cawp.rutgers.edu.

———. 2020c. "2020 Summary of Potential Women Candidates." Center for American Women in Politics. www.cawp.rutgers.edu.

———. 2020d. "Women in Congress: Leadership Roles and Committee Chairs." Center for American Women in Politics. www.cawp.rutgers.edu.

———. 2020e. "Women in Elective Office." Center for American Women in Politics. www.cawp.rutgers.edu.

———. 2020f. "Women in State Legislatures." Center for American Women in Politics. www.cawp.rutgers.edu.

———. 2020g. "Women in the U.S. Senate." Center for American Women in Politics. www.cawp.rutgers.edu.

Chambers, Stefanie, and Laurel Elder. 2020. "Ilhan Omar: Breaking Barrier for Muslim, Somali American and Immigrant Women." Paper presented at the annual meeting of the American Political Science Association, San Francisco, CA, September 10–13.

Chavez, Aida. 2019. "A Group of Progressive Women Just Launched a Working-Class Version of Emily's List." *The Intercept*, November 3. www.theintercept.com.

Childs, Sarah, and Mona Lena Krook. 2006. "Should Feminists Give Up on Critical Mass? A Contingent Yes." *Politics & Gender* 2 (4): 522–530.

Cho, Sumi, Kimberlé Williams Crenshaw, and Leslie McCall. 2013. "Toward a Field of Intersectionality Studies: Theory, Applications, and Praxis." *Signs* 38 (4): 785–810. doi:10.1086/669608.

Congressional Research Service. 2020. Profile of the 116th Congress. Updated June 1, 2020. https://fas.org.

Connolly, Griffin. 2018. "Republicans Aren't Including Minorities or Women, Say Two Minority Republican Women." *Roll Call*, December 14. www.rollcall.com.

Cooper, Betsy, Daniel Cox, Rachel Lienesch, and Robert P. Jones. 2016. "The Divide over America's Future: 1950 or 2050?" PRRI. www.prri.org.

Cooperman, Rosalyn, and Melody Crowder-Meyer. 2018. "A Run for Their Money: Republican Women's Hard Road to Campaign Funding." In *The Right Women: Republican Party Activists, Candidates, and Legislators*, edited by Malliga Och and Shauna L. Shames, 107–130. Denver Praeger.

Cornwell, Susan. 2019. "Republican Women Aim to Grow Their Numbers in U.S. House Next Year." *Reuters*, July 19. www.reuters.com.

Council of Economic Advisers. 2014. *White House Report: Women's Participation in Education and the Workforce*. https://obamawhite house.archives.gov.

Cox, Elizabeth M. 1996. *Women State and Territorial Legislators, 1895–1995*. Jefferson, NC: McFarland.

Crenshaw, Kimberlé. 1989. "Demarginalizing the Intersection of Race and Sex: A Black Feminist Critique of Antidiscrimination Doctrine, Feminist Theory and Antiracist Politics." *University of Chicago Legal Forum* 1989 (1): 139–167.

Crowder-Meyer, Melody. 2013. "Gendered Recruitment without Trying: How Local Party Recruiters Affect Women's Representation." *Politics & Gender* 9 (3): 390–413.

Crowder-Meyer, Melody, and Rosalyn Cooperman. 2018. "Can't Buy Them Love: How Party Culture among Donors Contributes to the Party Gap in Women's Representation." *Journal of Politics* 80 (4): 1211–1224. doi:10.1086/698848.

Crowder-Meyer, Melody, and Benjamin E. Lauderdale. 2014. "A Partisan Gap in the Supply of Female Potential Candidates in the United States." *Research and Politics* 1 (1): 1–7. https://doi .org/10.1177/2053168014537230.

Dann, Carrie. 2018. "Poll: Dems—More Than GOP—Say Country Would Be Better Off with More Elected Women." NBC News, June 7.

Darcy, R., Susan Welch, and Janet Clark. 1994. *Women, Elections and Representation*. 2nd ed., rev. Lincoln: University of Nebraska Press.

Day, Sharon. 2014. "RNC Co-chairman Sharon Day Delivers Remarks at the RNC 'Taking Back the Future' Women's Summit." Washington, DC, July 11. http://www.gop.com.

Dayen, David. 2018. "DCCC Injects Itself into a Third Texas Democratic Primary, This Time Going Up against EMILY's List." *The Intercept*, March 27. www.theintercept.com.

Deckman, Melissa. 2016. *Tea Party Women: Mama Grizzlies, Grassroots Activists, and the Changing Face of the American Right*. New York: NYU Press.

Desmarais, Bruce A., Raymond J. La Raja, and Michael S. Kowal. 2015. "The Fates of Challengers in US House Elections: The Role of Extended Party Networks in Supporting Candidates and Shaping Electoral Outcomes." *American Journal of Political Science* 59 (1): 194–211.

DiSalvo, Daniel. 2012. "The Great Reverse Migration: African Americans Are Abandoning the Northern Cities That Have Failed Them." *Pittsburgh Post-Gazette*, September 30. www.post-gazette.com.

Dittmar, Kelly. 2015. "Encouragement Is Not Enough: Addressing Social and Structural Barriers to Female Candidate Recruitment." *Politics & Gender* 11 (4): 759–765.

———. 2019. "Unfinished Business: Women Running in 2018 and Beyond." New Brunswick, NJ: Center for American Women and Politics, Eagleton Institute of Politics. www.cawp.org.

Dittmar, Kelly, Kira Sanbonmatsu, and Susan J. Carroll. 2018. *A Seat at the Table: Congresswomen's Perspectives on Why Their Presence Matters*. New York: Oxford University Press.

Dodson, Debra L. 2001. "Acting for Women: Is What Legislators Say, What They Do?" In *The Impact of Women in Public Office*, edited by Susan J. Carroll, 225–242. Bloomington: Indiana University Press.

Dolan, Kathleen. 2003. *Voting for Women: How the Public Evaluates Women Candidates*. Boulder, CO: Westview Press.

Dowe, Pearl K. Ford. 2016. "African American Women: Leading Ladies of Liberal Politics." In *Distinct Identities: Minority Women in U.S. Politics*, edited by Nadia E. Brown and Sarah Allen Gershon, 65–78. New York: Routledge.

Drusch, Andrea. 2014. "GOP PAC Targets Young Women." *Politico*, January 14. www.politico.com.

Elazar, Daniel J. 1984. *American Federalism: A View from the States*. 3rd ed. New York: Harper and Row.

Elder, Laurel. 2004. "Why Women Don't Run: Explaining Women's Underrepresentation in America's Political Institutions." *Women & Politics* 26 (2): 27–56.

———. 2008. "Whither Republican Women: The Growing Partisan Gap among Women in Congress" *The Forum* 6 (1): Article 13. http://www.bepress.com.

———. 2012. "The Partisan Gap among Women State Legislators." *Journal of Women, Politics & Policy* 33 (1): 65–85.

———. 2014a. "Contrasting Party Dynamics: A Three Decade Analysis of the Representation of Democratic versus Republican Women State Legislators." *Social Science Journal* 51 (3): 377–385.

———. 2014b. "Whither Republican Women in New England?" *New England Journal of Political Science* 7 (2): 161–193.

———. 2018. "Why So Few Republican Women in State Legislatures?" In *The Right Women: Republican Party Activists, Candidates, and Legislators*, edited by Malliga Och and Shauna L. Shames, 157–175. Santa Barbara, CA: Praeger.

Elder, Laurel, and Brian Frederick. 2019. "Why We Love Michelle: Understanding Public Opinion towards First Lady Michelle Obama." *Politics & Gender* 15 (3): 403–430. https://doi.org/10.1017/S1743923X19000436.

Elder, Laurel, and Steven Greene. 2012. *The Politics of Parenthood: Causes and Consequences of the Politicization and Polarization of the American Family*. Albany, NY: SUNY Press.

———. 2016. "Red Parents, Blue Parents: The Politics of Modern Parenthood." *The Forum: A Journal of Applied Research in Contemporary Politics* 14 (2): 143–167. doi:10.1515/for-2016–0013.

Elder, Laurel, Steven Greene, and Mary-Kate Lizotte. Forthcoming. "Feminist and Anti-feminist Identification in 21st Century United States." *Journal of Women & Politics*.

Fadel, Leila. 2019. "A First: Women Take the Majority in Nevada Legislature and Colorado House." NPR, February 4. www.npr.org.

Fording, Richard C. 2018. "State Ideology Data." https://rcfording.com.

Fox, Lauren, Ted Barrett, and Elizabeth Landers. 2017. "McConnell Defends Senate Health Care Group That Had No Female Members." CNN, May 9. www.cnn.com.

Fox, Richard. 2014. "Congressional Elections: Women's Candidacies and the Road to Gender Parity." In *Gender and Elections*, 3rd ed., edited by Susan J. Carroll and Richard L. Fox, 187–209. New York: Cambridge University Press.

———. 2018. "Congressional Elections: Women's Candidacies and the Road to Gender Parity." In *Gender and Elections*, 4th ed., edited by Susan J. Carroll and Richard L. Fox, 198–219. New York: Cambridge University Press.

Fraga, Bernard L., and Hans J. G. Hassell. 2020. "Are Minority and Women Candidates Penalized by Party Politics? Race, Gender and Access to Party Support." *Political Research Quarterly*. https://doi.org/10.1177/1065912920913326.

Frederick, Brian. 2009. "Are Female House Members Still More Liberal in a Polarized Era? The Conditional Nature of the Relationship between Descriptive and Substantive Representation." *Congress and the Presidency* 36 (2): 181–202.

———. 2011. "Gender Turnover and Roll Call Voting in the US Senate." *Journal of Women, Politics & Policy* 32 (3): 193–210.

———. 2013. "Gender and Roll Call Voting Behavior in Congress: A Cross-Chamber Analysis." *American Review of Politics* 34 (1):1–20.

Freeman, Jo. 1986. "The Political Culture of the Democratic and Republican Parties." *Political Science Quarterly* 101 (3): 327–356.

———. 1993. "Feminism versus Family Values: Women at the 1992 Democratic and Republican Conventions." *PS: Political Science & Politics* 26 (1): 21–27.

———. 1997. "Change and Continuity for Women at the Republican and Democratic National Conventions." *American Review of Politics* 18 (Winter): 353–367.

———. 1999. "Sex, Race, Religion and Partisan Realignment." In *"We Get What We Vote For . . . Or Do We?" The Impact of Elections on Governing*, edited by Paul E. Scheele, 167–190. Westport CT: Praeger.

Fry, Richard. 2019. "U.S. Women Near Milestone in the College Educated Workforce." Pew Research Center, June 20. www.pewresearch.org.

Frymer, Paul. 1999. *Uneasy Alliances: Race and Party Competition in America*. Princeton, NJ: Princeton University Press.

Garcia Bedolla, Lisa, Katherine Tate, and Janelle Wong. 2014. "Indelible Effects: The Impact of Women of Color in the U.S. Congress." In *Women and Elective Office: Past, Present and Future*, 3rd ed., edited by Sue Thomas and Clyde Wilcox, 235–252. New York: Oxford University Press.

Gay, Claudine, and Katherine Tate. 1998. "Doubly Bound: The Impact of Gender and Race on the Politics of Black Women." *Political Psychology* 19 (1): 169–184.

Gershon, Sarah Allen. 2012. "When Race, Gender, and the Media Intersect: Campaign News Coverage of Minority Congresswomen." *Journal of Women, Politics & Policy* 33 (2): 105–125.

Gertzog, Irwin N. 2002. "Women's Changing Pathways to the U.S. House of Representatives." In *Women Transforming Congress*, edited by Cindy Simon Rosenthal, 95–118. Norman: University of Oklahoma Press.

Gonzalez-Ramirez, Andrea. 2019. "Exclusive: New Hampshire's Maggie Hassan to Chair the Women's Senate Network." *Refinery29*, February 12. www.refinery29.com.

Grey, Sandra. 2006. "Numbers and Beyond: The Relevance of Critical Mass in Gender Research." *Politics & Gender* 2 (4): 492–501.

Grossmann, Matt, and David A. Hopkins. 2015. "Ideological Republicans and Group Interest Democrats." *Perspectives on Politics* 13:119–139.

———. 2016. *Asymmetric Politics: Ideological Republicans and Group Interest Democrats*. New York: Oxford University Press.

Haberman, Maggie, Jonathan Martin, and Nicholas Fandos. 2020. "White House Worries about Kelly Loeffler's Senate Prospects in Georgia." *New York Times*, May 22. www.nytimes.com.

Heldman, Caroline, and Lisa Wade. 2011. "Sexualizing Sarah Palin: The Social and Political Context of the Sexual Objectification of Female Candidates." *Sex Roles* 65 (3): 156–164.

Henderson, Nia-Malika, and Jackie Kucinich. 2014. "GOP See Progress, More Work on Gender Gap." *Washington Post*, March 17. www.washingtonpost.com.

Hetherington, Marc J., Meri T. Long, and Thomas J. Rudolph. 2016. "Revisiting the Myth: New Evidence of a Polarized Electorate." *Public Opinion Quarterly* 80 (S1): 321–350. doi.org/10.1093/poq/nfw003.

Hetherington, Marc, and Jonathan Weiler. 2018. *Prius or Pickup? How the Answers to Four Simple Questions Explain America's Great Divide*. Boston: Houghton Mifflin Harcourt.

Hicks, William D., Carl E. Klarner, Seth C. McKee, and Daniel A. Smith. 2018. "Revisiting Majority-Minority Districts and Black Representation." *Political Research Quarterly* 7 (2): 408–423.

Hill, David. B. 1981. "Political Culture and Female Political Representation." *Journal of Politics* 43 (1): 159–168.

Hogan, Robert E. 2001. "The Influence of State and District Conditions on the Representation of Women in U.S. State Legislatures." *American Politics Research* 29 (1): 4–24.

Holman, Mirya. 2019. "Women in Local Government: What We Know and Where We Go from Here." *State and Local Government Review* 49 (4): 285–296.

Hooghe, Marc, and Ruth Dassonneville. 2018. "Explaining the Trump Vote: The Effect of Racist Resentment and Anti-immigrant Sentiments." *PS: Political Science & Politics* 51 (3): 528–534.

Hook, Janet. 2014. "Aguilar-Reyes Primary Battle in California Is Test for Democrats." *Wall Street Journal*, April 27. www.wsj.com.

Hunt, Albert R. 2014. "Despite Leaps, Women Lag in Politics." *New York Times*, March 16. nytimes.com.

Hunt, Swanee. 2019. "What Happens When Women Rule." CNN, June 8. www.cnn.com.

Jacobson, Gary. 2015. "Obama and the Nationalized Electoral Politics in the 2014 Midterm." *Political Science Quarterly* 130 (1): 1–25.

———. 2019. "Extreme Referendum: Donald Trump and the 2018 Midterm Elections." *Political Science Quarterly* 134 (1): 9–38. https://doi.org/10.1002/polq.12866.

Jardina, Ashley. 2019a. "White Consciousness and White Prejudice: Two Compounding Forces in Contemporary American Politics." *The Forum* 17 (3): 447–466. doi:10.1515/for-2019–0025.

———. 2019b. *White Identity Politics*. Cambridge: Cambridge University Press.

Johnson, Eliana. 2017. "Big GOP Donors Launch Group to Elect Republican Women." *Politico*, October 25. www.politico.com.

Johnson, Sharon. 2013. "GOP Faces Uphill Effort in Electing More Women." *We-news*. November 18. www.womensenews.com.

Jones, Sarah. 2019. "Progressive Groups Back Marie Newman, Despite DCCC Blacklist." *The Intelligencer*, May 6. www.theintell.com.

Junn, Jane. 2017. "The Trump Majority: White Womanhood and the Making of Female Voters in the US." *Politics, Groups, and Identities* 5 (2): 343–352.

Kaufmann, Karen M. 2006. "The Gender Gap." *PS: Political Science & Politics* 39 (3): 447–453.

Kaufmann, Karen M., and John Petrocik. 1999. "The Changing Politics of American Men: Understanding the Sources of the Gender Gap." *American Journal of Political Science* 43 (3): 864–887.

Kawashima-Ginsberg, Kei. 2018. "The Other 2018 Midterm Wave: A Historic Ten-Point Jump in Turnout among Young People." *The Conversation*, November 8. www.theconversation.com.

Key, V. O. 1949. *Southern Politics in State and Nation*. Knoxville: University of Tennessee Press.

Kitchens, Karen E., and Michele L. Swers. 2016. "Why Aren't There More Republican Women in Congress? Gender, Partisanship, and

Fundraising Support in the 2010 and 2012 Elections." *Politics & Gender* 12 (4): 648–676. doi:10.1017/S1743923X1600009X.

Kittilson, Miki Caul, and Kim Fridkin. 2008. "Gender, Candidate Portrayals, and Election Campaigns: A Comparative Perspective." *Politics & Gender* 4 (3): 371–392.

Klinkner, Philip A., and Thomas F. Schaller. 2006. "A Regional Analysis of the 2006 Midterms." *The Forum* 4 (3): Article 9. doi:10.2202/1540–8884.1143.

Koger, Gregory, Seth Masket, and Hans Noel. 2009. "Partisan Webs: Information Exchange and Party Networks." *British Journal of Political Science* 39 (3): 633–653.

Kurtz, Karl. 2015. "Who We Elect: The Demographics of State Legislatures." *State Legislatures Magazine*, December 1. National Conference of State Legislatures. www.ncsl.org.

Lawless, Jennifer L., and Richard L. Fox. 2010. *It Still Takes a Candidate: Why Women Don't Run for Office*. Cambridge: Cambridge University Press.

———. 2018. "A Trump Effect? Women and the 2018 Midterm Elections." *The Forum* 16 (4): 569–590. doi.org/10.1515/for-2018-0038.

Lawless, Jennifer L., and Kathryn Pearson. 2008. "The Primary Reason for Women's Underrepresentation? Reevaluating the Conventional Wisdom." *Journal of Politics* 70 (1): 67–82.

Livingston, Abby. 2014. "House GOP's Effort to Elect More Women Gets Mixed Results." *Roll Call*, April 28. www.rollcall.com.

Love, Mia. 2018. "Mia Love: Republicans Have Failed to Bring Out Message to Minorities. It's Hurting the Nation." *Washington Post*, December 12. www.washingtonpost.com.

Lublin, David. 2018. "Eight White Majority Districts Elected Black Members of Congress This Year: That's a Breakthrough." *Washington Post*, November 19. www.washingtonpost.com.

Lynch, Timothy. 2017. "Temp to Perm: Stacking the Electoral Deck through U.S. Senate Appointments?" *Congress and the Presidency* 44 (3): 369–386. doi:10.1080/07343469.2017.1354944.

Maestas, Cherie D., L. Sandy Maisel, and Walter J. Stone. 2005. "National Party Efforts to Recruit State Legislators to Run for the U.S. House." *Legislative Studies Quarterly* 30 (2): 277–300.

Mansbridge, Jane. 1999. "Should Blacks Represent Blacks and Women Represent Women? A Contingent 'Yes.'" *Journal of Politics* 61 (3): 628–657.

Martin, Mart. 2001. *The Almanac of Women and Minorities in American Politics 2002*. Boulder, CO: Westview Press.

Matland, Richard E., and David C. King. 2006. "Women as Candidates in Congressional Elections." In *Women Transforming Congress*, edited by Cindy Simon Rosenthal, 119–145. Norman: University of Oklahoma Press.

Mayhew, David R. 1986. *Placing Parties in American Politics*. Princeton, NJ: Princeton University Press.

McKee, Seth C., and Melanie J. Springer. 2015. "A Tale of 'Two Souths': White Voting Behavior in Contemporary Southern Elections." *Social Science Quarterly* 96 (2): 588–607.

Mimms, Sarah. 2013. "Republicans Confront Lady Problems in Congress." *National Journal*, August 6. www.nationaljournal.com.

Mosbergen, Dominique. 2016. "Female Republican Lawmakers Slam Indiana Abortion Bill as 'Overreaching'; House Approved It Anyway." *Huffington Post*, March 11. www.huffingtonpost.com.

Murphy, Brian, and Dawn Baumgartner Vaughn. 2020. "As Voters, Black Women Are Important to Democrats. As Candidates, Where's the Support?" *News and Observer*, February 24. www.newsobserver.com.

Nagourney, Adam, and Kate Zernike. 2006. "In GOP Fund-Raising, Dole's Star Power Dims." *New York Times*, July 23. www.nytimes.com.

NALEO. 2018. "Election 2018: Elections to Watch: Post Election Results/State Races." https://d3n8a8pro7vhmx.cloudfront.net.

NBC. 2019. "More Republican Women Than Ever Are Planning to Run for Office." August 26. www.nbc.com.

NCSL. 2015. "The Term Limited States." National Conference of State Legislatures. March 13. www.ncsl.org.

———. 2019a. "Female Legislative Leaders 2018." National Conference of State Legislatures. March 22. www.ncsl.org.

———. 2019b. "Former State Legislators in the 116th Congress." National Conference of State Legislatures. www.ncsl.org.

———. 2020a. "Female Legislative Leaders 2020." National Conference of State Legislatures. January 16. www.ncsl.org.

———. 2020b. "State Partisan Composition." National Conference of State Legislatures. March 31. www.ncsl.org.

———. 2020c. "Women in State Legislatures for 2020." National Conference of State Legislators. January 7. www.ncsl.org.

Newton-Small, Jay. 2014a. "Female House Candidates Struggle to Break Through Despite GOP Efforts." *Time*, April 20. www.time.com.

———. 2014b. "Republicans Struggle to GROW Women in Recruitment Drive." *Time*, February 27. www.time.com.

Niven, David. 1998. "Party Elites and Women Candidates: The Shape of Bias." *Women and Politics* 19 (2): 57–80.

———. 2006. "Throwing Your Hat Out of the Ring: Negative Recruitment and the Gender Imbalance in State Legislative Candidacy. *Politics & Gender* 2 (4): 473–489.

Norrander, Barbara, and Clyde Wilcox. 2005. "Change in Continuity in the Geography of Women State Legislatures." In *Women and Elective Office: Past, Present and Future*, 2nd ed., edited by Sue Thomas and Clyde Wilcox, 176–196. New York: Oxford University Press.

———. 2014. "Trends in the Geography of Women in the U.S. State Legislatures." In *Women and Elective Office: Past, Present and Future*, 3rd ed., edited by Sue Thomas and Clyde Wilcox, 273–287. New York: Oxford University Press.

NPR. 2018. "First Latina Elected to Congress Retires with a Warning to Republicans." December 14.

Och, Malliga. 2018. "The Grand Old Party of 2016." In *The Right Women: Republican Party Activists, Candidates, and Legislators*," edited by Malliga Och and Shauna L. Shames, 3–24. Denver: Praeger.

O'Keefe, Ed. 2012. "Gillibrand Works to Elect More Women." *Washington Post*, August 11. www.washingtonpost.com.

Ondercin, Heather L., and Susan Welch. 2005. "Women Candidates for Congress." In *Women and Elective Office: Past, Present, and Future*, 2nd ed., edited by Sue Thomas and Clyde Wilcox, 60–80. Oxford: Oxford University Press.

O'Regan, Valerie, and Stephen J. Stambough. 2014. "Female Governors and Gubernatorial Candidates." In *Women and Elective Office, Past, Present and Future*, 3rd ed., edited by Sue Thomas and Clyde Wilcox, 147–161. New York: Oxford University Press.

———. 2018. "Term Limits and Women's Representation: A Democratic Opportunity and a Republican Dead-End." *Politics, Groups, and Identities* 6 (4): 650–665. doi:10.1080/21565503.2016.1256819.

Osborne, Tracy. 2012. *How Women Represent Women: Political Parties, Gender and Representation in the State Legislatures*. New York: Oxford University Press.

Osborne, Tracy, and Rebecca Kreitzer. 2014. "Women State Legislators: Women's Issues in Partisan Environments." In *Women and Elective Office: Past, Present and Future*, 3rd ed., edited by Sue Thomas and Clyde Wilcox, 181–198. New York: Oxford University Press.

Palmer, Barbara, and Dennis Simon. 2006. *Breaking the Political Glass Ceiling: Women and Congressional Elections*. New York: Routledge.

Paru Shah, Jamil Scott, and Eric Gonzalez Juenke. 2019. "Women of Color Candidates: Examining Emergence and Success in State Legislative Elections." *Politics, Groups, and Identities* 7 (2): 429–443. doi:10.1080/21565503.2018.1557057.

Pathe, Simone. 2016. "Democrats Aim to Reduce 30 Seat House Deficit with Help from Trump." *Roll Call*, June 20. www.rollcall.com.

———. 2018. "Elise Stefanik Wants to Play in Primaries to Help Republican Women." *Roll Call*, December 8. www.rollcall.com.

———. 2019. "Brooks Wants More Republican Women to Run in 2020, Even If She Won't." *The Hill*, June 17. www.thehill.com.

Paxton, Pamela, Matthew A. Painter II, and Melanie M. Hughes. 2009. "Year of the Woman, Decade of the Man: Trajectories of Growth in Women's State Legislative Representation." *Social Science Research* 38 (1): 86–102.

Pear, Robert. 2017. "13 Men, and No Women, Are Writing New G.O.P. Health Bill in Senate." *New York Times*, May 8. www.nytimes.com.

Pearson, Kathryn, and Logan Dancey. 2011. "Speaking for the Underrepresented in the House of Representatives: Voicing Women's Interests in a Partisan Chamber." *Politics & Gender* 7 (4): 493–519.

Petrocik, John. 1987. "Realignment: New Party Coalitions and the Nationalization of the South." *Journal of Politics* 49 (2): 347–375.

Pew Research Center. 2013. "Modern Parenthood." March 13. www.pewsocialtrends.org.

———. 2014. "Political Polarization in the American Public." June 12. www.people-press.org.

———. 2019. "Blacks Have Made Gains in U.S. Political Leadership, but Gaps Remain." January 18. www.people-press.org.

Philpot, Tasha S., and Hanes Walton. 2007. "One of Our Own: Black Female Candidates and the Voters Who Support Them." *American Journal of Political Science* 51 (1): 49–62.

Preuhs, Robert R., and Eric Gonzalez Juenke. 2011. "Latino US State Legislators in the 1990s: Majority-Minority Districts, Minority Incorporation, and Institutional Position." *State Politics & Policy Quarterly* 11 (1): 48–75.

Puglise, Nicole. 2015. "GOP Women's Recruitment Effort Adapts for 2016." *Roll Call*, July 6. www.rollcall.com.

Railey, Kimberly. 2014. "Republicans Gain Little Ground among Women." *Boston Globe*, March 26. www.bostonglobe.com.

Ransford, Paige, Carol Hardy-Fanta, and Anne Marie Cammisa. 2007. "Women in New England Politics." *New England Journal of Public Policy* 22 (1): 17–36.

Reingold, Beth. 2019. "Gender, Race/Ethnicity, and Representation in State Legislatures." *PS: Political Science & Politics* 52 (3): 426–429.

Reingold, Beth, Rebecca Kreitzer, Tracy Osborn, and Michele L. Swers. 2015. "Antifeminism and Women's Representation in the States." Paper presented at the annual meeting of the American Political Science Association, San Francisco, CA, September 3–5.

Republican National Committee. 2013. The Growth and Opportunity Project.

Rosin, Hanna. 2014. "Values Feminism: Cathy McMorris Rodgers, Supermom, Is the New Model for a Successful Republican Woman." *Slate Magazine*, January 28. www.slate.com.

Rowe, Abigail. 2018. "The Parity Paradox." *Best Lawyers: Women in the Law*, June 25. www.bestlawyers.com.

Rule, Wilma. 1999. "Why Are More Women State Legislators?" In *Women in Politics: Outsiders or Insiders?*, 3rd ed., edited by Lois Duke Whitaker, 190–202. Upper Saddle River, NJ: Prentice Hall.

Sakelaris, Nicholas. 2019. "DCCC's New Director Has Experience Getting Democratic Women Elected." UPI, September 12. www.upi.com.

Sanbonmatsu, Kira. 2002. "Political Parties and the Recruitment of Women to the State Legislatures." *Journal of Politics* 64 (3): 791–809.

———. 2004. *Democrats/Republicans and the Politics of Women's Place.* Ann Arbor: University of Michigan Press.

———. 2006. *Where Women Run: Gender and Party Politics in the American States.* Ann Arbor: University of Michigan Press.

———. 2015. "Electing Women of Color: The Role of Campaign Trainings." *Journal of Women, Politics & Policy* 36 (2): 137–160. doi:10.10 80/1554477X.2015.1019273.

———. 2018. "Women's Election to Office in the Fifty States: Opportunities and Challenges." In *Gender and Elections: Shaping the Future of American Politics*, 4th ed., edited by Susan J. Carroll and Richard L. Fox, 280–302. New York: Cambridge University Press.

Sanbonmatsu, Kira, and Kathleen Dolan. 2009. "Do Gender Stereotypes Transcend Party?" *Political Research Quarterly* 62 (3): 485–494.

Sarasohn, David. 2013. "The Most Underestimated Feminist." *The Nation*, June 4. www.thenation.com.

Schreiber, Ronnee. 2014. "Conservative Women Candidates." In *Women and Elective Office: Past, Present, and Future*, 3rd ed., edited by Sue Thomas and Clyde Wilcox, 111–125. New York: Oxford University Press.

Schuller, Rebecca. 2019. "Yes, the GOP Has a Woman Problem—Yes, It Can Be Solved." *The Hill*, July 26. www.thehill.com.

Scola, Becki. 2013. "Predicting Presence at the Intersections: Assessing the Variation in Women's Office Holding across the States." *State Politics & Policy Quarterly* 13 (3): 333–348.

———. 2014. *Gender, Race, and Office Holding in the United States: Representation at the Intersections.* New York: Routledge.

Shames, Shauna. 2017. *Out of the Running: Why Millennials Reject Political Careers and Why It Matters.* New York City: NYU Press.

———. 2018. "Higher Hurdles for Republican Women: Ideology, Inattention, and Infrastructure." In *The Right Women: Republican Party Activists, Candidates, and Legislators*, edited by Malliga Och and Shauna L. Shames, 95–106. Denver: Praeger.

Silva, Andrea, and Carrie Skulley. 2019. "Always Running: Candidate Emergence among Women of Color over Time." *Political Research Quarterly* 72 (2): 342–359.

Simien, Evelyn. 2007. "Doing Intersectionality Research: From Conceptual Issues to Practical Examples." *Politics & Gender* 3 (2): 264–271.

———. 2015. *Historic Firsts: How Symbolic Empowerment Changes US Politics*. New York: Oxford University Press.

Smooth, Wendy. 2006. "African American Women and Electoral Politics: Journeying from the Shadow to the Spotlight." In *Gender and Elections: Shaping the Future of American Politics*, edited by Susan J. Carroll and Richard L. Fox, 117–142. New York: Cambridge University Press.

———. 2013. "Intersectionality from Theoretical Framework to Policy Intervention." In *Situating Intersectionality: Politics, Policy and Power*, edited by Angela R. Wilson, 11–41. New York: Palgrave Macmillan.

———. 2018. "African American Women and Electoral Politics: The Core of the New American Electorate." In *Gender and Elections: Shaping the Future of American Politics*, 4th ed., edited by Susan J. Carroll and Richard L. Fox, 171–197. New York: Cambridge University Press.

Stambough, Stephen J., and Valerie R. O'Regan. 2007. "Republican Lambs and the Democratic Pipeline: Partisan Differences in the Nomination of Female Gubernatorial Candidates." *Politics & Gender* 3 (3): 349–368.

Stokes-Brown, Atiya Kai, and Kathleen Dolan. 2010. "Race, Gender, and Symbolic Representation: African American Female Candidates as Mobilizing Agents." *Journal of Elections, Public Opinion and Parties* 20 (4): 473–494. doi:10.1080/17457289.2010.511806.

Storey, Tim. 2016. "What Election 2016 Meant for State Legislatures." *State Legislatures Magazine*, December 1. www.ncsl.org.

Strolovitch, Dara Z., Janelle S. Wong, and Andrew Proctor. 2017. "A Possessive Investment in White Heteropatriarchy? The 2016 Election and the Politics of Race, Gender, and Sexuality." *Politics, Groups, and Identities* 5 (2): 353–363.

Swers, Michele L. 2002. *The Difference Women Make: The Policy Impact of Women in Congress*. Chicago: University of Chicago Press.

———. 2013. *Women in the Club: Gender and Policy Making in the Senate*. Chicago: University of Chicago Press.

———. 2014. "Representing Women's Interests in a Polarized Congress." In *Women and Elective Office: Past, Present, and Future*, 3rd ed., edited by Sue Thomas and Clyde Wilcox, 162–179. New York: Oxford University Press.

———. 2016. "Pursuing Women's Interests in Partisan Times: Explaining Gender Differences in Legislative Activity on Health, Education, and Women's Health Issues." *Journal of Women Politics and Policy* 37 (3): 249–273.

———. 2018. "From the Republican Revolution to the Tea Party Wave: Republican Women and the Politics of Women's Issues." In *The Right Women: Republican Party Activists, Candidates, and Legislators*, edited by Malliga Och and Shauna L. Shames, 199–228. Santa Barbara, CA: Praeger.

Swers, Michele L., and Carin Larson. 2005. "Women in Congress: Do They Act as Advocates for Women's Issues?" In *Women and Elective Office, Past, Present, and Future*, 2nd ed., edited by Sue Thomas and Clyde Wilcox, 110–128. Oxford University Press.

Tate, Katherine. 1994. *From Protest to Politics: The New Black Voters in American Elections*. Enl. ed. Cambridge, MA: Harvard University Press and the Russell Sage Foundation.

———. 1997. "African American Female Senatorial Candidates: Twin Assets or Double Liabilities?" In *African American Power and Politics*, edited by Hanes Walton Jr. 264–281. New York: Columbia University Press.

———. 2003. *Black Faces in the Mirror: African Americans and Their Representatives in the U.S. Congress*. Princeton, NJ: Princeton University Press.

Thomas, Sue. 1994. *How Women Legislate*. New York: Oxford University Press.

Thomsen, Danielle M. 2013. "Fed Up with Congress? Then Help Elect More Republican Women." *Washington Post*, December 3. www.washingtonpost.com.

———. 2014. "Ideological Moderates Won't Run: How Party Fit Matters for Partisan Polarization in Congress." *Journal of Politics* 76 (3): 786–797.

———. 2015. "Why So Few (Republican) Women? Explaining the Partisan Imbalance of Women in the U.S. Congress." *Legislative Studies Quarterly* 40 (2): 295–323.

———. 2017. *Opting Out of Congress: Partisan Polarization and the Decline of Moderate Candidates*. New York: Cambridge University Press.

Thomsen, Danielle M., and Michele L. Swers. 2017. "Which Women Can Run? Gender, Partisanship, and Candidate Donor Networks." *Political Research Quarterly* 70 (2): 449–463.

Trygstad, Kyle. 2010. "Super Tuesday's Under-the-Radar Races." *Real Clear Politics*, June 8. www.realclearpolitics.com.

Tumulty, Karen. 2019. "Female Representation Matters: Colorado's Legislature Proves That." *Washington Post*, April 12. www.washingtonpost.com.

Uhlaner, Carole Jean, and Becki Scola. 2015. "Collective Representation as a Mobilizer." *State Politics & Policy Quarterly* 16 (2): 227–263. doi:10.1177/1532440015603576.

Usha Ranji, Yali Bair, and Alina Salganicoff. 2016. "Medicaid and Family Planning: Background and Implications of the ACA." Kaiser Family Foundation. February 3. http://kff.org.

Volden, Craig, Alan E. Wiseman, and Dana E. Wittmer. 2013. "When Are Women More Effective Lawmakers Than Men?" *American Journal of Political Science* 57 (2): 326–341.

Ward, Orlanda. 2016. "Seeing Double: Race, Gender, and Coverage of Minority Women's Campaigns for the U.S. House of Representatives." *Politics & Gender* 12: 317–343.

Warshaw, Christopher. 2019. "Local Elections and Representation in the United States." *Annual Review of Political Science* 22 (1): 461–479.

Williams, Ben. 2018. "West Virginia Moves to Single Member Districts." *The NCSL Blog*, April 10. www.ncsl.org.

Wineinger, Catherine. 2018. "Gendering Republican Party Culture." In *The Right Women: Republican Party Activists, Candidates, and Legislators*, edited by Malliga Och and Shauna L. Shames, 25–49. Denver: Praeger.

———. 2019. "How Can a Black Woman Be a Republican? An Intersectional Analysis of Identity Claims in the 2014 Mia Love Campaign." *Politics, Groups and Identities*. https://doi.org/10.1080/21565503.2019.1629316.

Wineinger, Catherine, and Mary K. Nugent. 2020. "Framing Identity Politics: Right-Wing Women as Strategic Party Actors in the UK and US. *Journal of Women, Politics & Policy* 41 (1): 91–118.

Winter, Nicholas J. G. 2010. "Masculine Republicans and Feminine Democrats: Gender and Americans' Explicit and Implicit Images of the Political Parties." *Political Behavior* 32:587–618.

Wolbrecht, Christina. 2000. *The Politics of Women's Rights: Parties, Positions, and Change*. Princeton, NJ: Princeton University Press.

Wong, Janelle S. 2019. "Race, Evangelicals and Immigration." *The Forum* 17 (3): 403–419. doi:10.1515/for-2019–0031.

Zhou, Li. 2020. "Why More Republican Women Are Running for the House Than Ever Before." *Vox*, May 27. www.vox.com.

INDEX

ABOUT THE AUTHOR

LAUREL ELDER is Professor of Political Science at Hartwick College. She is the coauthor of *American Presidential Candidate Spouses: The Public's Perspective* and *The Politics of Parenthood: Causes and Consequences of the Politicization and Polarization of the American Family.*